HOW TO MAKE YOUR DOLLS' HOUSE SPECIAL

FRESH IDEAS FOR DECORATING

HOW TO MAKE YOUR DOLLS' HOUSE SPECIAL

FRESH IDEAS FOR DECORATING

BERYL ARMSTRONG

GUILD OF MASTER CRAFTSMAN PUBLICATIONS

First published 2000 by
Guild of Master Craftsman Publications Ltd,
166 High Street, Lewes,
East Sussex BN7 1XU
Copyright © GMC Publications Ltd 2000
Text © Beryl Armstrong 2000
ISBN 1 86108 182 0

A catalogue record of this book is available from the British Library.

Project editor: Nicola Wright
Copy editor: Rosie Hankin
Book designer: Jane Hawkins
Cover designer: Ian Smith
Photographer: Nick Nicholson
Line illustrations: Penny Brown
Typeface: Lapidary
Colour separation: Viscan Graphics (Singapore)
Printed in Hong Kong by H&Y Printing Ltd

10 9 8 7 6 5 4 3 2 1

Dolls' house blank on front cover from Colchester Toy Shop, UK

CONTENTS

INTRODUCTION

West Green Manor. My first special house which I made without any plans, kit, experience or help

MILLIONS OF DOLLS' HOUSES have been made all over the world but only the best will survive as heirlooms. It is up to you, the creator, to present a miniature that is sturdy, attractive and unique. The effect can be simple or elaborate – the choice is yours.

Whether you build the house yourself, or from a kit or buy ready-made, the finish is the deciding factor; however the choice of materials and methods is daunting. You can buy virtually everything you need ready-made by master crafts people but this can be expensive as you are paying for their time and expertise. However, even the inexperienced amateur can achieve good results at low cost with a little guidance and by learning a few tricks of the trade.

I don't try to imitate the professionals. I do my own thing to the best of my ability using methods that are simple and cheap yet produce sound and attractive results. By the time you have read this book and tried a few of my projects I hope you too will be on your way to developing your own creations. You will then have the skills to make a dolls' house which reflects your personality.

DIY is time consuming but our hobby is a craft that gives a purpose in life and considerable satisfaction. Here you will find a wide choice of ideas so you can decide which method is best for you and the style or period you consider most attractive.

For the purposes of this book, I am assuming that you are starting with your house still in the basic wood or MDF board without any of the fittings such as windows, doors, stairs and fireplaces, or internal and external decoration.

Right: A country farmhouse can have many interesting features

ANYONE CAN DO IT

A dolls' house is merely a box divided into rooms so building one is really quite simple. However, many enthusiasts, when they have the basic carcass of their house, whether it has been bought ready-made or built from a kit, abandon their project because the finishing appears too daunting. My reconstructed house is at this stage. How you decorate your house is your choice. I shall give you many ideas to inspire you that are easy to do or make and don't cost a fortune. It only takes a few simple changes at minimal cost to make a basic house into something special. Here are some examples.

- Tongue depressors from the chemist, lollipop sticks, imitation household bricks, sandpaper and a few lengths of stripwood were the only materials required to transform a child's toy into a country station museum. I added a waiting room and garden to lengthen the platform and complete the picture. It is one of my most popular exhibits with the public.

This kit was sold as a child's toy

Just a few alterations transformed a child's toy into a typical country station museum

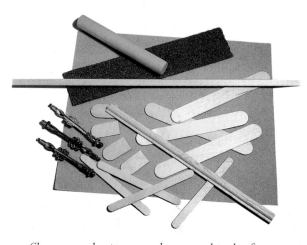

Cheap, everyday items can have a multitude of uses

The kit opened at the back so the museum has to be seen from both sides. A disadvantage when exhibiting but it is always popular

- A fancy tissue box cut into a balcony and verandah enhanced a small house which is basically two stacked room boxes.

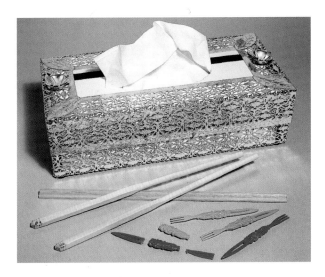

A tissue box holder, chopsticks, takeaway forks and stripwood gave me ideas to decorate the flint house opposite

- I have increased the appeal of my tiny corner shop simply by standing it on a baseboard and adding a garden and street scene – which I furnished mainly with items made from recycled odds and ends.

I had fun furnishing this gift shop, but the outside was too basic and small

A cart bought from a charity shop triggered the idea for a street scene

- I built up the extended front of a Victorian shop to form a tower, removed the roof and added crenellations. With a stone effect on the outside it became a unique castle with a museum of old armoury downstairs and royalty upstairs.

When this kit was built it lost its original appeal so...

...I transformed it into a castle where I could house my showcase of crown jewels and a collection of armour. This museum is a favourite with young boys

This is the kit house's original specification

The original rear view. The house opened at the back and had internal design faults

A while ago I was given a half-made kit abandoned by the owner. This particular house had design faults in that the staircase and double-width front doors were in the kitchen and, as it was an American kit, it opened at the back. This left just one wall for fittings in that room.

The challenge was to put a covered staircase outside the main building and extend the original front of the house to give a larger kitchen and bedroom using the balcony space. In doing so I could utilize the area under and behind the stairs to create a lobby. Rear-opening houses are often impractical so I made a new front on the back. This meant replacing the roof to create usable rooms where doors could be added.

All this reconstruction entailed using odd pieces of wood and plaster filler so I gave the whole house a coat of primer to cover the defects and to seal the wood before decoration.

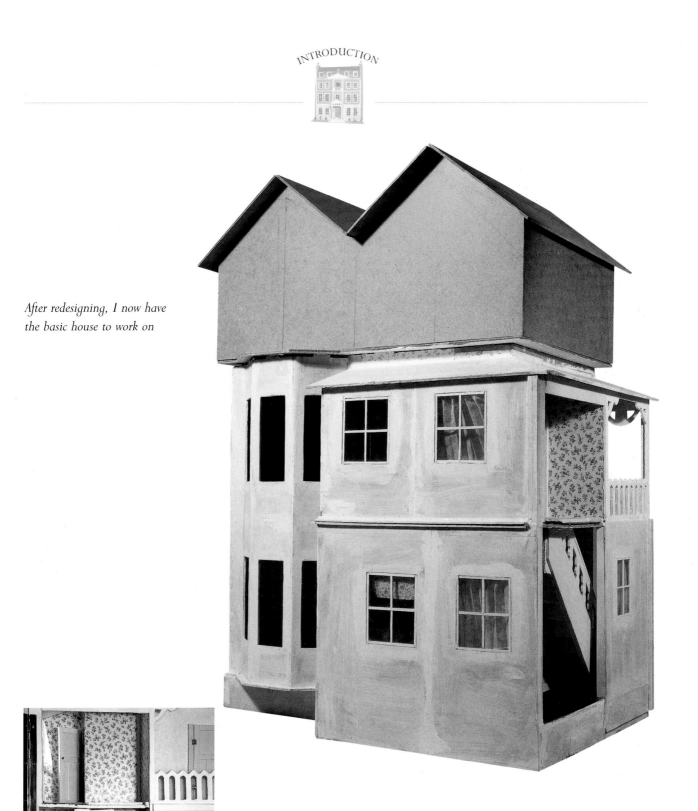

After redesigning, I now have the basic house to work on

When redesigning a house, think ahead. I had to finish decorating the staircase area before adding the outer walls

TOOLS AND MATERIALS

For every job specific tools are required. However, good results can be achieved with the simplest of tools that need not cost very much. If you buy your basic dolls' house ready-made, most of the big tools won't be needed. If you want to treat yourself then I would suggest a vibratory scrollsaw which is versatile and the most valued of all my big tools.

The projects I have suggested in this book need little more than a craft knife, small saw, power/hand drill, Archimedes drill, wide steel ruler, set square, tweezers and scribe. Any other tools required will be stated within each project.

GLUES

A plethora of glues for every type of material is available. Often the same glue has a different brand name. Each of you will have your favourite or you may be restricted by what your local shops sell.

PVA wood glue is fine for every type of wood and board but being water based it will cause warping on very thin wood. It can be diluted to any degree for pasting paper or as a varnish, but not for anything white as it discolours.

Tacky Glue is widely available under various brand names. It is water based and will join many different types of material. It is the choice for fabrics; it dries clear and flexible. Diluted to various degrees, it can also be used for paper and as a varnish.

UHU is spirit based and should be used for joining non-absorbant materials like plastic or metal to wood. This dries clear and is preferred where it is likely to show, such as bricking, on window glazing bars and for adding moss to roofs.

Impact adhesive is strong for any feature likely to be under stress such as chimneys and door hinges. It is my choice for roof tiles and the like because it doesn't warp the wood. If used wet it gives you time to adjust the position and it sets fairly quickly compared to a water-based wood glue. It is available in tubes and works out cheaper for intermittant use as it will remain fluid. It dries as a discoloured gum so

should not be considered if an overflow is likely to show. There is a non-drip impact adhesive which I used for the thatching but it is only available in tins and unless you are using it in one session, it dries hard and then the remainder is wasted.

Superglue is widely advertised but personally I don't like it, but others find it invaluable for tiny spot attachments.

VARNISHES AND POLISHES

A shellac sand sealer is ideal for filling in the wood grain to give a smooth surface for polishing. It gives a semi-matt sheen and if you rub the wood down with fine steel wool you will end up with a silky feel.

If you want a high shine such as on furniture or wall panelling then I use French polish after first using the sealer. Ordinary household furniture and boot polish also have their uses.

PAINTS

Paints are used extensively but which type to use? Wide areas of gloss paint make a doll's house look larger than 1:12 scale. A vinyl silk emulsion is suitable for most jobs but vinyl matt is preferable for roof tiles and bricks. You can rub down gloss with fine steel wool to give it a light sheen or apply a semi-varnish to matt paint for the same effect.

WOOD

Some woods are suitable while others are inadvisable. Quality birch ply is expensive but preferable for a surface that needs to be smooth for painting, such as doors. A cheaper ply has a rougher surface, is more liable to warp and gives untidy grooves for simulating planks, but worth considering if it is to be covered with any form of rendering.

MDF (multi-density fibre board) is widely used now, mainly because it is cheap, easy to saw and has a smooth surface. However, the fibres often show up after painting and screws do work loose under stress points, for example on hinges. It's useful if covered with tiles or bricks.

Grain is another important factor as it is not always in our scale. Oak is not recommended but mahogany, obeche and fruit woods give good results.

GENERAL HINTS AND TIPS

• You can join odd woods into larger sheets. In remaking the kit house I have used all types of wood and MDF, especially on the roof. Providing they are the same thickness and you have a perfectly flat surface you can glue the pieces together. Try to apply pressure on the side to keep the edges firmly in contact. Once dry, you can cut the patched sheet to the required size.

• Plastic wood seems to dry even in an airtight tube after the first use. Save your sawdust and sieve it into a fine powder. This can be mixed to a fairly thin paste with PVA glue and a few drops of water then used like plastic wood. Be aware that it dries rock hard and can be difficult to sand so keep it within the area to be filled.

• Most people replace cutting boards when the groove becomes too deep. Fill the gaps with plastic wood to create a smooth surface.

• Plaster filler, like mustard, creates a lot of waste. For small quantities mix it in a spoon.

• Warped ply is a problem especially if it is cheap. It often warps when it is painted or pasted one side only. Straighten ply by wetting both sides, clamping it firmly to a flat bench and leaving it to dry for several days.

• In the past the wood was cut by hand; today it is machine-cut so the corners are sharp. Lightly sand the edges and corners on your dolls' house woods to give a more realistic appearance.

• To fill the wood grain before polishing or painting, use a shellac sanding sealer. It also gives a matt varnish. You will need methylated spirit to clean the brushes.

- A flat strip of soft wood broken to a wedge is a useful tool for removing excess glue. When removing spirit glue from Perspex, wait until the glue is slightly set but not dry.

- Keep your old artist's brushes that have just a few hairs remaining. These are useful for small spot touching-up, for example on glazing bars.

- A flat artist's brush is easier to use than a round one.

- Use your finger for applying small areas of glue and plaster filler. It gives a far superior spread and greater control. Your skin is waterproof and cleans easily with soap, white spirit, lighter fuel (petrol) or worn sandpaper. Apply some hand-cream after cleaning.

- Many kits recommend using a glue gun. Unless you are experienced with this tool, don't use it. It can leave ugly random globules which makes doing a neat job on a building even more difficult.

- You can buy a variety of metal or plastic clamps but there are times when it is more practical to use elastic bands, insulating or masking tape, pegs and Lego blocks (to keep corners square).

- When building a dolls' house always think ahead to avoid problems. For example, is it simpler to add curtain fittings before you glue on the ceiling? Should you fit the door and its architraves before you fix the fireplace?

- If you have used scrap woods and a lot of filler to save money or when remaking a dolls' house, a plain coat of paint over the top would show up the imperfections. Cover the surface with wallpaper and rendering for a more professional finish.

CHAPTER ONE

FIREPLACES AND SURROUNDS

The fireplace is the most eye-catching feature in a room

IT IS ALWAYS preferable to work on the inside of a dolls' house first. To give you confidence I will start with something simple. Fireplaces are not actually required until you come to the wallpapering stage but they have to be ready in advance. They provide a good introduction to creating interior features for your house.

FIRE BASKET

Plastic hair rollers come in all shapes and sizes and are a useful standby for making many items.

1 Take a medium-size roller with square holes and strip off the comb protrusions so you have a smooth surface. Also cut off the thick ends and their tags.

2 Count five holes down and cut right across the diameter. Stand it on end and make two more cuts vertically downwards so you have six holes round. You end up with a curved section that is six holes on the curve and five on its length. Remove all the excess tags and the centre two holes along its length but not the outer rims. You now have a curved section with a slit in the middle which will be the basket to hold the fire.

3 For its base, take the remaining piece of roller, count five holes and cut right through so you are left with four holes after removing the tags. Again make vertical cuts so you have six holes on the round. This time remove two rows of holes on its length on each side of the outer edges, but do not cut the outermost ribs because these are the four legs.

4 Glue the upper basket to the base, paint the whole piece black and it is now ready for a wood or coal fire.

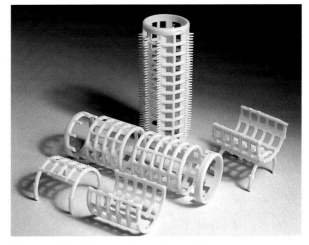

Use a craft knife to cut plastic hair rollers

The basket has a slit down the middle

The base has the outer sections removed to form the legs

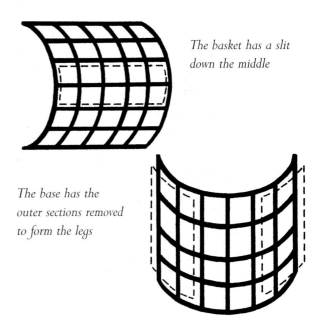

FIRE-BACK

An embossed tin lid makes an ideal fire-back

Like hair rollers, string has many uses, especially for embossed decoration. You can of course buy exquisite fire-backs, authentic in every detail. This is fine if you are anticipating an empty fireplace so your fire-back will be seen. However, with a lit fire much of the fire-back will be hidden, so make your own which will look just as good and will be much cheaper.

1 Cut out the fire-back shape (suggested outline opposite) from a piece of ¹⁄₁₆in (1.5mm) ply or card. Whether you make it tall and slim or wide and short will depend on the size of your open fireplace.

2 Using a cocktail stick or your finger, pipe a ribbon of Tacky Glue or PVA wood glue all round the outer edge on the front. Press into this a thin piece of smooth string. If your string is too thick,

separate the strands and, stretching it out first, use just one strand.

3 The centre of the fire-back can be decorated with whatever small pieces of costume jewellery you have. Other alternatives include patterns cut from a plastic doily, the branched tips of an artificial Christmas tree or petals taken from plastic flowers. Shapes punched from thin card are also acceptable. Don't use anything too thick as it must look as though the rim and motifs have been cast from iron with the backplate as a whole. The embossed lid of a plastic or tin box can also make a good fire-back in a large open fire grate like those seen in stately homes.

4 Paint your fire-back black or gunmetal grey. I use black emulsion followed by a coat of light varnish.

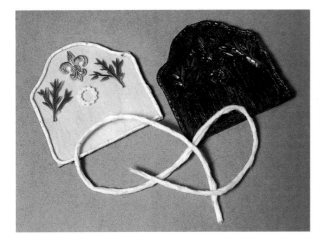

A piece of wood or card, string and motifs are used to make this fire-back

Simple materials can be used to make realistic fireplaces

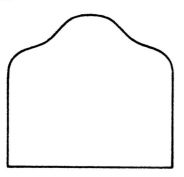

Suggested fire-back template

TIP If, like me, you are no artist, make accurate curves for any piece of furniture using round pots, dishes and saucers, according to the size of curve you need. For the fire-back I used a plastic film container to draw around. A pair of compasses will also come in handy when curves need to be very accurate.

FIRE GRATE

Early stove grates were free-standing and often replaced the original open log fire where so much of the heat was lost up the wide chimney.

During the Industrial Revolution the first iron foundries manufactured stove grates from smelted ore converted to wrought iron. Abraham Darby, who moved to Coalbrookdale in Shropshire in 1708, pioneered the smelting of iron by using coke. The resultant hotter molten iron was of such a high quality that it could be poured into enclosed moulds capable of producing much finer castings. The detailed motifs were mainly of a neo-classical style. Grates were now set into the flue. Because this threw more heat into the room it became the design of choice during the late eighteenth century.

If you plan to have fireplaces in the bedrooms, they can be made quite effectively using a similar method to the fire-back.

STOVE GRATE

1 Trace the pattern provided on to $\frac{1}{16}$in (1.5mm) ply or card. As long as the cut-outs are in the right place, you could make the plate a little wider or you can take it right to the ceiling in one piece. This will then form the front of your chimney breast.

2 As explained for the fire-back (see page 16), pipe a ribbon of Tacky Glue or PVA all round the front edge of both the cut-outs and along the bottom, but not across the top of the upper hole because this is the place where you will fit a mantel shelf. This is the point where you start to pipe glue down each side of the plate.

3 Press a thin piece of smooth string into the glue. If your string is too thick, separate the strands and, stretching it out first, just use one strand. A second strand just round the two cut-outs is optional, but will enhance the appearance of the grate.

4 For the motifs use whatever pieces of costume jewellery you have. I have also used pieces cut from a plastic doily and Christmas tree. Don't use any material that is too thick as it must look as though the rim and motifs have been cast from iron with the front plate as a whole.

5 For the front fire bars take a suitable thickness of black plastic-covered flex. Cut three graded lengths about $\frac{1}{2}$in (13mm) wider than the width of the hole. Strip off the plastic by $\frac{1}{4}$in (6mm) from each end of each wire.

Right: String, wire and plastic caps will give you an authentic fireplace

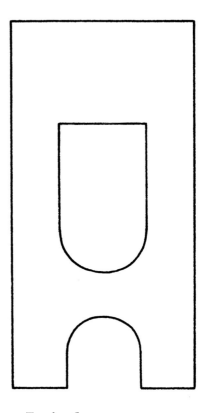

Template for stove grate

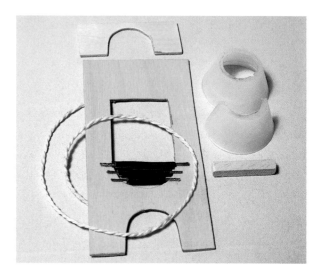

6 Starting at the base of the upper curve, glue the bared wire ends of the shortest length inside the front plate. You will need a strong glue and tweezers are useful for manipulating the wire into position. Fix all three fire bars in place with the top wire level with the position for the top plate.

7 For the fire baskets I used conical plastic caps (these also make useful lampshades). I discovered these in a cycle shop. They are used as hub protectors during transit between factory and shop and are then thrown away. For mini-maniacs just about anything discarded by others can be turned into something useful. If you cannot find these caps, try using plastic bottle caps or even a section of a hair roller. When filled with wood or coal and a red lamp, not much will be visible. Cut the plastic cap vertically in half. The widest diameter should be the same as the width of the upper hole in your fire plate. If you cannot find a basket to fit, then cut a fresh front plate with the upper hole made to match your container.

8 When the two fit nicely together, glue the basket to the back of the fire plate so the curve is level with the curve of the hole. Again you will need a strong glue to make sure the basket is fixed over the wire ends. I usually glue a short piece of beading under the plastic as a support. This piece can be carved to make a cradle if you wish.

9 Now stick the top plate section (cut from the pattern provided overleaf) to the top of the basket. Cut this piece again to fit neatly over your chosen basket if it is a different size.

10 Paint your fireplace in black and set it into your chimney breast, adding a mantle shelf before wallpapering.

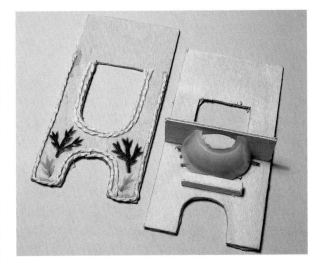

Front and back views of the fireplace

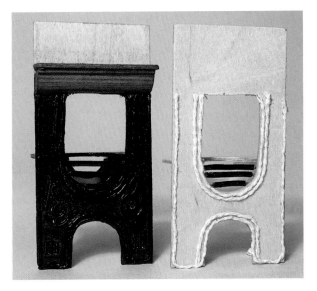

A few motifs and black paint complete your stove grate front

TIP A fine nozzle hobby syringe applicator is even more efficient than using a cocktail stick or your finger when piping a ribbon of glue.

HOB GRATE

Hob grates are basically a variation on the stove grate

Hob grates were so called because the fire bars were flanked by hobs which extended to the sides from the front plate on a level with the top bar. These provided a useful surface on which to boil a kettle. During the Industrial Revolution there were three designs called Bath, Pantheon and Forest, depending on the shape of the front plates. They were more often installed in the less important rooms downstairs, though I have seen some in bedrooms. In the nursery, for example, one essential was a boiling kettle to create steam for children suffering from croup. You can make a hob grate with just a little variation to the stove grate.

Which grate you choose is a matter of room size. The stove grate is made as an integral part of the chimney breast, around 2in (50mm) wide. By contrast, the Forest hob grate slides into a fireplace which is built separately and is therefore wider.

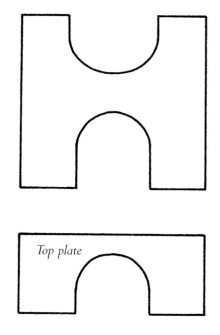

Top plate

Template for the free-standing Forest hob grate

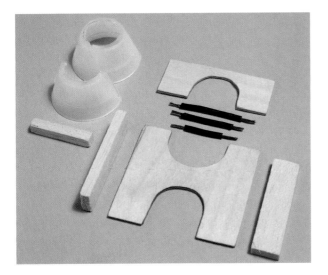

Components for hob grate

There are many alternatives for decoration

1 Cut the front plate down to the top of the plastic basket so the hob can sit on top.

2 To make the stove stand upright, glue two strips of beading behind to form legs.

CHIMNEY BREAST

The design for my chimney breast is made from a strip of ¹⁄₁₆in (1.5mm) ply or card the width of your fireplace, usually about 2¼in (57mm) wide and as high as your ceiling measures from the floor. The side walls are about 1in (25mm) deep and again go up to the ceiling. When glued to the front breast it forms a box-like structure. Stripwood or balsa inside helps to strengthen the chimney breast. If you have opted for the short front plate then you will have to glue an extended piece of ply to make the whole reach up to the ceiling. An alternative to the box of ply is to make the entire chimney breast from a solid piece of balsa wood.

TIP Drill a hole on the far side wall, wide enough to take a bulb and holder for the firelight. The wiring will then be run down the far wall of the chimney breast and soldered into the floor circuit.

The stove grate set into a box-shaped chimney breast

KITCHEN RANGE SURROUND

In the early Middle Ages, cooking in grand households took place on the floor of the central hall. The grate was little more than an area of clay tiles placed on edge and set into the earth floor. The smoke escaped through a hole in the roof.

By the early seventeenth century the open hall had been divided into two with extra bays added at either end. A massive brick chimney stack was built round the central partition. Cooking was still done on the open fire but now a variety of cooking aids could be used, including chains, pulleys, bottle-jacks and roasting spits.

As time went by, brick or metal ovens were built to one side of the big open fireplace. Flues were directed round the oven to prevent heat loss up the wide chimney. With the first iron foundries any number of patents appeared as each company developed its own ideas for a cooking range.

For the dolls' house enthusiast the stove most often favoured is the closed range with an oven to the left, hot water tank to the right and the fire in the centre. Flues, dampers and top plates control the heat. These cooking ranges were therefore cleaner and the original open fire with its wide chimney stack had become a tailor-made unit.

The width of your chimney breast/cooking range will depend on the size of your kitchen, and the surround I have designed can be adapted to your needs. I suggest you buy your stove first and build the surround to fit. In theory, only stately homes and large households would have had such an elaborate set-up with warming cupboards and a roasting spit. However, I enjoy the fun side rather than being absolutely authentic, so my Sussex farmhouse has all but the spit.

A kitchen range complete with stove, plate rack and warming cupboard with sliding doors

A plate rack was quite common even in the most primitive homes. If you don't want warming cupboards, simply leave them out. However, the same sliding door cupboards made as a separate unit could also be used above a wardrobe, below a shelf unit or counter or in an alcove, so there's no harm in having a go at all the elements of this kitchen surround.

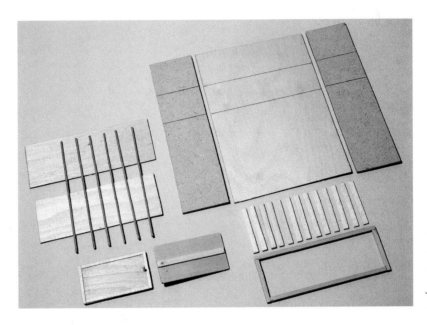

*Components
needed for the
range surround
showing doors
front and back
ready-made*

As with the stove grates you make the range unit and then add the chimney breast to fit your room. It is most likely to be painted in black so any cheap wood or card is practical. The thickness is not critical except for the sliding doors and runners.

Sides – 2¾in (70mm) high x 1¾in (44mm) wide.
Back – 2¾in (70mm) high x 4½in (113mm) wide or approximately ½in (12mm) wider than your stove. This can be thinner wood than that used for the sides e.g. ¹⁄₁₆in (1.5mm) ply.
Plate rack – stripwood approximately ⅛in (3mm) square for the frame.
Slats – ¹⁄₁₆in (1.5mm) thick x approximately ⅛in (3mm) wide.

The outer measurements of the basic plate-rack frame must correspond to the width of your back panel and the depth of your side walls, less the thickness of the back. This sounds complicated but just remember that the side walls will be glued to the edges of the back panel which sits inside. In my

example I used ¹⁄₁₆in (1.5mm) ply so the sides of the plate-rack frame will allow for this. It is easier to make the rack first because it helps keep your carcass square when it is glued together. The slats can be left until later.

1 Draw lines across the back and sides of the carcass to leave a 2¾in (70mm) clear space above the plate rack. Add another line 1¼in (32mm) above this for the floor of the cupboard.

2 Glue the side edges of the back panel and three sides of the plate-rack frame and assemble with the side walls.

3 Now you can add the slats. The two outer slats are glued to the side walls and the frame to give stability. How many you lay across from front to back will depend on the width of your surround and whether you want to have plates piled or slotted upright between the slats.

Detail of the plate rack and warming cupboard

WARMING CUPBOARD WITH SLIDING DOOR

1 Cut a piece of $\frac{1}{16}$in (1.5mm) ply to sit inside your surround so it leaves a $1\frac{1}{4}$in (32mm) space above the plate rack. This is the bottom of your cupboard, but it is easier to add the runners while the floor is still on the work bench, and also to adjust the position when you fit the doors.

2 The roof of the unit is cut to sit on top of the sides and back but do not glue this in place yet. Use it as a guide for measuring the height of your doors.

3 The runners are made from $\frac{1}{8}$in (3mm) square stripwood. Cut and glue a length the full width of your floor and right to the front. Cut five more to this length but do not glue them yet until you have made your doors.

4 For the doors use $\frac{1}{16}$in (1.5mm) ply. Each door is $\frac{1}{4}$in (6mm) wider than half your unit width so they slightly overlap. In my example it measured $2\frac{1}{2}$in (64mm) because my back panel was $4\frac{1}{2}$in (113mm). The height is the gap you have left between the cupboard floor and the top lid.

5 Around the front edges only on each door, glue a frame of stripwood. This is about $\frac{1}{8}$in (3mm) wide and wafer thin. A piece of greetings card would do. The idea is to make it look like a door frame and also to give a little depth. The door knobs are pieces of cocktail stick glued inside the mini-frame.

6 Glue a piece of thin $\frac{1}{4}$in (6mm) stripwood behind each door across the centre. This gives extra purchase for the door knobs which are glued into drilled holes. This strip also acts as a stop when the door is slid open to prevent it banging against the other knob. Paint the doors black back and front.

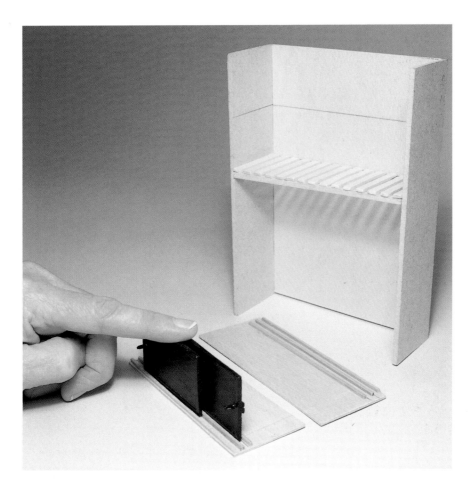

Use your doors to gauge where to glue the runners

7 Fitting the runners is perhaps the only tricky part of the whole unit. Take the cupboard floor with its one piece of stripwood at the front. Stand one of your doors upright behind and touching this runner. Lay another runner behind the door and stand the second door behind this. Now you have to judge where to glue the second runner so the doors don't jam. In practice it is the thickness of one door plus a minute clearance gap. The centre strip behind each door is the width of a runner so you don't have to allow extra for this.

8 Glue the second and third runners with a corresponding gap. Usually there is time before the glue hardens to make minor adjustments.

10 On the underside of the roof, glue your three other runners to correspond with the floor runners.

11 Glue the floor in place. I glued another very narrow strip of wood across the back of the floor to give extra strength and support.

Before gluing the top, test that the doors work perfectly

12 Have a trial assembly run, but don't glue the top yet because you must paint the inside of the whole cupboard or it will remain as whitewood. When you are satisfied that the sliding doors work perfectly, glue the roof into position.

13 Paint the whole interior of the unit black. I usually blacken the outside as well, but to create a truly authentic chimney flue it should either have a surround added (you have to add a block above your unit to ceiling height anyway) or you can paint the outside as it stands to match your kitchen walls. When I have enough space in the kitchen I make cupboards to fit either side of the unit. These were quite common in houses.

14 A final touch would be a lining of tiles above the top of your range to below the warming cupboard. Don't forget to make the flue pipe and dampers on the back wall of the unit. I have deliberately left the bottom open. You can stand the unit on the kitchen floor, on a slab of tiles or on a raised stone hearth.

The side cupboards and shelf are not fixed to the unit making it easier to first position the fire surround with its stove in a narrow restaurant kitchen

SITTING-ROOM FIRE SURROUNDS

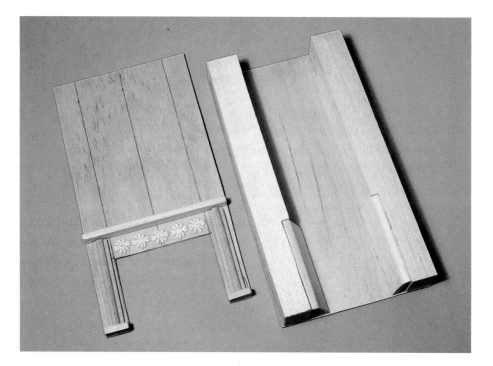

Basic assembly of a sitting-room fireplace. This simple suggestion uses balsa wood for the support and side walls

The most important room in the house is the sitting-room, and its fire surround deserves special treatment.

The average opening for a fire hearth is about 3in (75mm) wide, 2¼in (57mm) high and 1in (25mm) deep. This depth took up too much space in the kit house in my example so I had to reduce this to ¾in (19mm). The chimney breast can be any size you want. For example, if you are making an old stone or brick fireplace then the chimney breast will be much wider than, say, a fireplace in the study or morning room.

What material you use for your fire surround will depend on what you have to hand and whether it is to be plain or ornate. There are plenty of magazine photographs of fire surrounds for you to copy, with traders providing miniaturists with carved stripwood. Fans have useful filigree spines; plastic flowers and embroidered edging can also have their uses. If it is to be a stone or brick surround then see the relevant sections in Chapter Six for suggestions.

This alternative method was used in a previous house

1 Cut your front plate in ply as you did for the stove grate (see page 18), but make the opening more square-shaped – although some do have a curved front plate. The surround consists of two uprights, a cross piece and a mantle shelf.

2 The fire grate consists of a backplate higher than the opening. The side walls slope inwards at a slight angle between the surround and the backplate. Build your chimney breast round this.

3 The fireplace usually stands on a stone or tile base which protrudes into the room. Depending on the style, you can leave it as an open hearth or add a fender. Your hair-roller fire basket (see page 15) will complete the feature.

The fireplace I made for the kit-house sitting-room

In the manor, the fireplaces were all in the outside chimney flues, hence the surrounds are glued straight on to the walls

This fireplace was created for the study in my manor house – a typical gentleman's room, with his trophies, bookcases, desk and games table. Wood panelling (half or full height) and lots of wood features look appropriate in this room

An old cottage is complemented by a farmhouse-style brick fireplace. When creating a fireplace don't forget to blacken the inside where soot has been deposited on the brickwork over the years

My thatched cottage has a kitchen but all the cooking is done over the fire. The kettle, cauldron and saucepan were brass ornaments. The bottle-jack had a clockwork mechanism so meat hanging on the hooks would cook as the jack slowly turned (it can be easily made with a piece of tubing and wire hooks). I have added a metal oven in part of the extensive fireplace

CHAPTER TWO

WALLPAPERING

The best rooms in the house often had wallpaper panels

YOU NOW HAVE all your fireplaces completed so the next task is to decide where they are to be positioned in your dolls' house. They must be authentic, that is not under or over a window or door in another room. Each fire on each floor must have a common flue right up to the chimney on the roof. If there is no fire in one room, such as in the roof space, then you must make a false chimney flue over the fire on the floor below.

Stand your fires against the chosen walls and draw a pencil line down each side, then take them out again. These marks are a useful guide when wallpapering, especially if you have a style or pattern that has to be centred in an alcove.

The choice of wallpaper for a dolls' house is more important than for your own home. The whole house will be seen at once, so the colours must blend to give an overall attractive appearance. The patterns must always be in keeping with 1:12 scale. Authentic dolls'-house papers are plentiful but also expensive; however there are many household papers with small motifs to choose from. For a few pence part rolls can be bought at boot sales or scrounged from friends. Even some borders can be cut down and used as a dado or for panelling. Gift wrap is often worth considering but as these are rather thin they are more likely to tear or bubble. Real silk was used in some grand houses but again there is a knack in adhering this to your dolls' house to avoid ugly glue stains. Transfers come in every subject and can be very effective stuck on to plain painted paper. Likewise, coloured ink stamps can be used to create your own patterned wallpaper with curtains to match.

The choice of wallpaper for each room must take account of the need for overall colour harmonization

The sequence you adopt in wallpapering is important for a neat finish. If your staircase has not been fixed in place, so much the better; however, if it has, although it is harder to wallpaper round it, it will still be possible with a little extra know-how. I will begin by describing the simple procedure of straight wallpapering – without windows and doors in place – and then go on to the more advanced techniques and problem areas.

1 Start with the ceilings. Either paint with a silk emulsion to complement your chosen colour scheme or use a full-size embossed wallpaper to simulate plaster rendering. If you use a patterned wallpaper then you must measure carefully so you end up with a balanced ceiling. For example, can you use the centre of a rosette for a ceiling rose? If so then its position is vital.

2 Cut the paper to fit the ceiling with a wide margin for error. If it has a strong pattern then trim it down a fraction at a time round all the edges to keep the balance central and correct. When it is exactly the right size for your ceiling, use quite a thick paste to soak into the paper and also paste the wood ceiling.

3 You will find it much easier to work inside a room if you can lay your house on its back. Put your pasted paper in place and rub it down with a soft cloth, pressing well into the corners and along the edges. Work from the centre outwards to squeeze out excess paste and remove any bubbles. Go back every few minutes and apply pressure with your cloth. When dry you can either paint with emulsion or leave the paper plain white.

TIP   Minor crinkling and small bubbles will disappear as the paper dries but you have to be aware there could be larger areas which are unattached. If you are using anaglypta paper which is heavily embossed you also have to be careful not to press so hard that the pattern disappears.

Paper right over windows and door openings. When dry, cut away the excess. The back wallpaper should turn the corner by $\frac{1}{4}$in (6mm)

4 To make the instructions simpler I am assuming that your fires will be on the side walls. Starting on the back wall, cut your chosen paper about ½in (13mm) wider than your wall. Always paste both the paper and the walls before applying the paper. Press the paper well into the corners with an excess ¼in (6mm) on each side. This is to avoid an ugly gap appearing down your wall. Paper right over door and window holes which are still open and bare. The excess cuts away quite easily when the adhesive has dried and doing this avoids warping round the frame which often happens when the cutting is done before pasting. However, if your builder has already hung your doors you will have to cut round these openings.

5 For the side walls cut your paper to fit exactly, making sure you match up the pattern from the back so it carries on from wall to wall. If it protrudes slightly at the front, this can be trimmed with a craft knife when the paper is perfectly dry. Paste both wall and paper then press the sheet right into the corner so it covers the overlap from the back wall.

6 Take your chosen fireplace for that room. Paper the chimney breast, leaving a ¼in (6mm) flap on either side. This is to avoid an ugly join where it joins the main wall. Put it aside until required.

Top: The side paper goes right into the corner over the back wall flap. The join will be invisible if you've matched the pattern.

Bottom: Paper your fireplace leaving a flap on either side

If the far alcove has a window or door needing fixtures, do this work before gluing the fireplace

7 You need to take the paper that will cover the alcove on the far side of the chimney breast into the corner over the overlap from the rear wall and to the pencil line of your chimney breast. However, do not glue it right to the line because you will need to paste this paper over the flap on your chimney. If this area happens to have a window then I strongly advise you to glaze it now and also put up any fixtures like curtain rails. If you leave it until the chimney breast is in place, the job will be much more difficult.

8 Now you can glue in the chimney and fire using strong glue and tucking the rear flap under the rear alcove paper and pasting down the front flap. The paper for the front alcove is cut to butt up to the corner of the chimney over the flap to make a neat join.

ALTERNATIVE WALLPAPERING

If your house is an upmarket model, do you want the staterooms looking more exotic? One idea is to use silk but pasting this may damage the delicate material. Your best bet would be to cut thin card walls then stretch the silk over these to wrap round to the back where it can be glued. The false walls can then be glued to the room of the house.

Centre panels are another popular feature. Here you mark out the areas where the panels will be positioned. Cut the special paper to fit and cut the base paper to fit round the panel. Along the joins use a small beading previously painted or stained to build up a frame.

I have used gilt paper for the panels but artist's wall panels were often used. You could use postcards or magazine pictures if in the appropriate scale

WALLPAPERING AROUND A STAIRCASE

A straight edge down the stairs makes wallpapering simpler

If your builder has already glued the staircase in a small hall, wallpapering can be frustrating. You have to review the situation and decide whether painting or papering would give the best result. Whatever your decision you must see to the staircase first. Painting is no problem but if you want it stained then you have to assess if there is any leakage of glue over the treads or spindles. Stain will not soak into wood over glue.

Wallpapering down to the stair treads for a neat result is virtually impossible. The only solution is to find a narrow beading and glue it the full length of the stairs, touching the front treads all the way down. You now have a straight cut for the wallpaper. The gap between stairs and beading is stained or painted along with the staircase.

Another method I have used is to glue panelling on the wall from the treads up to the banister height. If you used ⅜in (8 or 10mm) stripwood about 3in (75mm) high laid closely side by side, you will have a look that is neat and easy to achieve. It leaves a more manageable job of wallpapering the upper wall.

CEILING ROSES

These can be made from modelling clay using crimped pastry cutters and shaped containers. The patterns are made with fancy buttons, retraction ball-pen insides and cocktail sticks.

Useful items for making ceiling roses

A small hook in the centre would hang chains for a shade (hair roller) or chandelier

Gold paint trim gives an ornate finish

PANELLING

Panelling can be made from various materials. A dado at waist height is often seen, with the lower 3in (75mm) separated from the upper wall with a strip of beading. For the lower half, on various houses, I have used paint, lightly embossed cartridge paper, commercial paper borders and wood panelling.

Wood panelling looks expensive but is quite simple to do. This can be for a whole wall, up to the picture rail or merely the lower half. Whatever height you choose the procedure is the same.

The following instructions are for plain divisions. If you want to be more ambitious and have raised dividing strips then choose the stripwood carefully. If the raised carving is gradual from edge to middle you would create an ugly join at each junction. You can overcome this by mitring these vertical strips to blend in with the horizontal.

Designer panelling looks special yet is so simple to achieve

Plain panelling is effective and you could add linenfold or plain raised centrepieces in each square

Designer panelling looks luxurious using shaped cut-outs and fancy stripwood while half-wall panelling is practical in a kitchen.

Gluing full-wall panels into the room can be tricky and needs firm pressure to make sure they stick evenly without warping. With your house on its back you can hold the rear panel with weights, always going back repeatedly to add finger pressure. Use a strong spirit glue as water-based adhesive will warp the thin ply. For the side panels I found it more difficult to create a strong pressure. I solved this by using wire coat hangers. They bend and can be sprung between the walls; using two or three gives even pressure but check every few minutes to make sure all is well.

Victorian kitchens often had half-walled panelling

1 Cut ⅟₃₂in (0.8mm) ply to the exact size of the area you want to panel. The divisions are made from ⅟₁₆in (1.5mm) obeche or other stripwood, using three different widths, approximately 6, 8 and 10mm. Stain all the wood before you start working.

2 Use the widest stripwood first and glue to the bottom of your panel for the skirting board. Glue the middle size right across the top, working it round any cut-outs for windows and also down each side from top to skirting.

3 Divide the panel into equal sections all the way down. The distance between them depends on the size of the square/rectangular panels you want to achieve. Take the narrow beading and glue lengths horizontally right across on the divisions you have marked.

4 The small vertical divisions have to be cut individually and spaced between the horizontal strips so that they form the square panels and are evenly spaced across the width. This means they may not be exact squares but the overall appearance must look uniform.

5 Restain the whole panel and polish. Make all the panels right round the room in the same way, if you wish. However, if you are butting ends together round the corner then you may need to use the wider beading down one edge so that when it tucks behind the adjoining wall it looks like the middle-size beading.

Make your panel to fit the wall exactly

TIP If you are planning a Georgian or Victorian room you may want just the lower half panelled and painted in cream or green. Glue the top, bottom and sides in the same manner but leave out the horizontal strips. The panels here will be much larger so the vertical strips will go from top to bottom. The back sheet can be cut from card if it is to be painted.

When turning a corner, use the wider stripwood to tuck behind the adjoining wall so that it looks like the middle-size beading

CHAPTER THREE

DOORS

This door is in my manor house. You'll have to decide what style would be appropriate for your house

Doors will vary according to the style of your dolls' house. It isn't always possible to take inspiration from our own homes because today many doors have been replaced with double-glazed units or other innovations. Books on historical buildings will give you appropriate guidance.

Panelled doors were the norm in upmarket houses

If your room dividers have not yet been glued into the house carcass then hinging a door is a lot easier. However, if they are fixed in place, then the choice of hinging is limited.

1 Place a piece of card – an old greetings card will do – behind the door opening and hold it firmly in position with a book or piece of wood. Draw round the opening then cut out the card template. This is necessary if your door openings are not accurate or the same size throughout your dolls' house.

2 Use the template to cut a wooden door using good quality ply about $\frac{1}{8}$in (3mm) thick.

TIP I build my houses using $\frac{1}{4}$in (6mm) ply, so make my doors in $\frac{1}{8}$in (3mm) ply. However many dolls' houses are made with $\frac{3}{8}$in (9mm) throughout, although I think this is excessively heavy and unnecessary especially for internal fittings. If you have $\frac{3}{8}$in (9mm) partitions, you will need to use, say, wood that is $\frac{5}{32}$in (4mm) thick for your doors.

Cutting a wooden door

3 Try your basic door for size, sanding down where necessary until it fits the doorway with a slight clearance at the sides and top and a little more at the bottom to allow for the floor covering. If you are going to use pin hinges rather than inset brass, you will have to allow for a bottom step (see page 49).

4 Now decorate your door. For a simple country-style door, gouge vertical grooves (use a metal ruler to ensure straight lines) in the ply to simulate planks. Quality ply is best or the wood will rough up. If you do not have a sharp gouge, use a fine screwdriver instead. Alternatively, glue beading to both sides leaving a minute gap between each length. These must of course, be stained first unless you intend to paint the door. Sand the edges of your sandwich and recheck that it still fits your doorway.

A simple country-style door

PANELLED DOORS

In upmarket houses, panelled doors were the norm. You will find it useful to study books on different styles of architecture to find which design was in vogue during your chosen period.

Start with the basic ply door as before and stain if required. Now glue $\frac{1}{16}$in (1.5mm) stripwood in the pattern you have chosen. Start with the vertical edges and fit the crossbars in between. For the panelling, use squares of $\frac{1}{16}$in (1.5mm) ply to fit the areas between the beading, leaving a small gap all round to simulate a router groove.

Adding the final panel

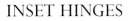

INSET HINGES

You will find it impossible to inset brass hinges when your dividing walls are in place. If they are not, this is what you would do.

1 Mark the position of your hinge on the door panel and on the wall edge surrounding it. Hold the door firmly in a vice and gouge a seating for the hinge no deeper than the thickness of the brass. You will also need to gouge a groove on the corresponding door frame.

2 Pin one side of the hinge to the door. Add a drop of impact glue before pinning as doors are subject to a lot of wear especially with children who find them irresistible.

Mark the position of your hinge on the door panel

Gouge a shallow seating for the hinge

Pin one side of the hinge to the door

3 Fold the hinge closed and put the door in position to see if the hinge matches the groove on the frame.

4 Clamp the room divider firmly to the bench with parcel or masking tape so the door will be at right angles and pre-drill holes in the ply edge. Then pin in the other half of the hinge, again applying a drop of glue behind it first. Impact glue is preferable to superglue because you can remove the hinge before it hardens if it is not quite right.

TIP Brass pins have flanges which often make it difficult to hammer through the hinge holes. Use a drill bit or fine round file to make the brass hole fractionally larger. It is also advisable to use a fine Archimedes drill to make a small hole in the wood before inserting the pin.

Pre-drill holes in the ply edge of the frame

Secure the door at right angles and pin the door hinge to the frame

External hinges are simple to achieve

EXTERNAL HINGES

If your room-dividing walls are fixed, the simple solution is to use external hinges.

1 Cut your door slightly larger all round than the opening.

2 Lay the hinges flat on the door, pinning the other half to a strip of wood that is the same thickness.

3 Glue the strip to the wall and your door is in place.

Dressmaker's pins are often used for hinges

PINNED DOORS

Another common method of hinging is with steel dressmaker's pins. This is quite simple and effective in most circumstances. If when you have hung your door it does not swing freely on its pivots, sand the hinge edge to make it slightly rounded.

1 Drill a fine hole in the top edge of the door as close to the corner as possible and make a corresponding hole in the door frame.

2 Press the pin into the door as far as it will go. Cut off the head and reverse the pin so you can poke the sharp point hard into the hole in the frame.

3 Insert another pin into the bottom edge of the door and cut off the head.

4 You will now have to make a doorstep that sits between the open frame to take the other end of the pin.

SLIDING DOORS

These are fun if you have large rooms or the house opens back and front with a two-room depth.

For a sliding door, you will need to make a second wall with a gap between the two using stripwood as spacers. The door slides between the walls. Remember to put a stop in the cavity so the door doesn't disappear. Otherwise you'll have to keep tipping the house on its side to bring the door out from between the two walls. It is not sensible to use the door knobs as stops because the constant opening will soon dislodge them.

Sliding doors save space and are practical if you have rooms behind

TIP   Remember to add doorknobs before inserting any of your doors. Also, bear in mind that there were no letter boxes on front doors in Britain before the Penny Post was introduced in 1840.

ARCHITRAVES

These are added after a room is wallpapered. Door and window architraves are cut at 45 degrees where they meet. Lining up the two sides against a column of newspaper print is a quick way of checking the angles. Another useful idea is to remove a sliver of wallpaper all round the doorway so it does not show on the edge of the glued architraves.

Right: Use newspaper columns as guides for checking mitres meet perfectly

Window and door architraves are mitred at 45 degrees

CHAPTER FOUR

FLOOR COVERINGS

An odd piece of wallpaper made this stylish floor. The wall tapestries were cut from a handbag

REMEMBER THAT FITTED CARPETS are a comparatively modern idea. In the old days large squares of carpet were used with polished wood floor surrounds.

In more humble homes small rugs on stone slabs, quarry tiles or bare boards predominated.

A patterned wallpaper stuck over thin card is a possibility for, say, a bathroom or kitchen. In the sculpture gallery featured here, I used a Roman-style wallpaper.

Some vinyl tiles make useful stone slabs. If the grain has deep holes then fill them in with plaster filler. The large tile is cut into squares or rectangles. Very lightly sand the edges to avoid a modern cut.

Vinyl tiles can be cut into paving slabs

Use impact glue to fix them to the floor and grout with filler. When painted, this filler looks a slightly different shade and therefore authentic, or you can paint it darker using a fine brush. This simulated stone floor is ideal for, say, the kitchen or hall on the ground floor where no wiring is used under it.

The upper rooms are most likely to have the wiring under them. These will probably be wood planking which you make after putting the skirting board in position. Suitably grained wallpaper can make an acceptable wooden floor when it is stained.

TIP Wiring or copper tape for lighting should never be placed behind the wallpaper or any other fixture. When things go wrong lighting should be accessible for repairs. If the bulbs burn out after a few years, finding the same wallpaper to replace the damaged areas may be impossible. So make sure your wiring is placed under removable floor coverings or behind false wall panels.

Medieval wooden floors had wider planks than, say, Victorian. So check your period and scale down accordingly

PLANK FLOOR

1 Cut ¹⁄₁₆in (1.5mm) stripwood – obeche wood is the most effective – into 6in (152mm) lengths.

2 Take a piece of fine-weave material, such as curtain lining, and cut it slightly larger than the room floor.

3 Using plenty of wood glue, glue the strips side by side to the material laid over newspaper. Make sure the joins are not all in the same line by first gluing to the depth of the room then butting the next row to the previous, starting from the opposite end. As the rooms will not be exactly 12in (305mm) you should get staggered joins.

4 Glue a length of stripwood the full width of the room at the front of the house. With a steel ruler and craft knife cut all the strips glued on your floor panel in a straight line to fit inside this fixed front piece. Re-stain the cut edge.

5 You will find that the whole floor on its material backing is very flexible. Taking one side at a time gradually cut the flooring to fit round any protrusions such as door architraves or fireplaces, not forgetting to re-stain all the cut edges.

The flooring can be held flat over the wiring by using heavy double-sided tape in between the wires. This is removable so you will be able to look at the lighting at any time, simply replacing with new tape afterwards.

Glue your planks to close-weave material like curtain lining

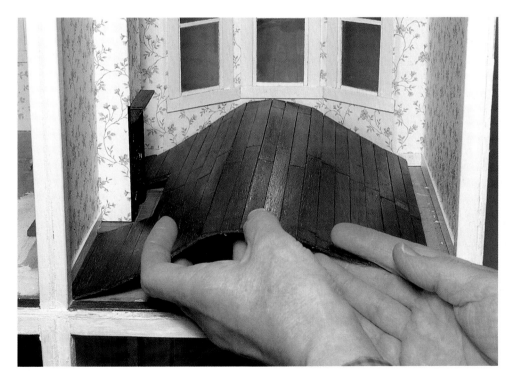

The floor panel is flexible and can be cut to fit round protrusions

BLACK AND WHITE TILED FLOOR

A black and white tiled floor can be simulated by using paper strips. Simply glue black and white strips alternately to a sheet of white paper. Turn the paper 90 degrees and cut the sheet into strips so the black and white squares alternate. Now glue these to yet another sheet of paper, moving the strips along so the squares alternate to give an overall black and white chequered floor.

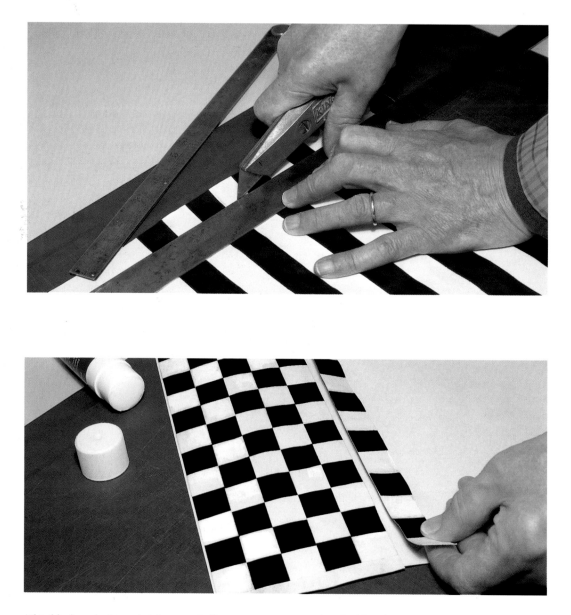

This black and white tiled floor made from paper was painted with diluted wood glue to give it a sheen

RED CLAY FLOOR

Stone slabs (vinyl tiles) for the kitchen and red clay tiles (squares of wood) for the country living room

The red clay tile floor can be simulated using ⅟₁₆in(1.5mm) ply cut into small squares. Grout as before and paint brick red. A final polish with brown shoe wax gives it an authentic surface.

CHAPTER FIVE

STAIRCASES

The staircase is a major feature in a dolls' house

Making a staircase always seems daunting to the novice but there are different ways of approaching the task. A lot depends on the width of your hallway and where the builder has cut the stairwell in the ceiling. The hardest part is adding the spindles and handrail, and adjusting the height as they near the ceiling. A straight staircase fixed to one wall is the simplest of all; however, whatever the design there are tips to make life easier.

TRIANGULAR WOOD METHOD

For a normal-size room you will need approximately 14 stairs cut from a strip of ³⁄₄in (19mm) triangular-shaped wood, available from most general DIY stores. The normal width of each stair is 2¼in (57mm) but this will be governed by the width of your stairwell hole. As stain is not absorbed by glue – it leaves blotchy patches if you apply after gluing – you must stain all component pieces before fixing in position. Stick the wide bases close together on a length of ¹⁄₁₆in (1.5mm) ply, 14in (354mm) long and 2¼in (57mm) wide.

Always stain wood before gluing

SOLID BLOCK STAIRCASE

Another popular approach is to stick solid blocks of wood on top of each other, each block set slightly back from the step beneath. This staircase is useful in a confined space where you need to adjust the treads to fit a limited depth into the room. I have used blocks for the front steps of the kit house shown.

Solid block staircases save space but using stringers, treads and risers is more professional

USING STRINGERS, TREADS AND RISERS

A more sophisticated method for making a staircase is to use stringers, treads and risers, as in real life. You can buy stringers but you can also make your own.

1 Cut two stringers from $\frac{1}{8}$in (3mm) thick wood using the full-size pattern from the diagram provided here.

2 The stair treads should measure $\frac{7}{8}$in (22mm) deep by $2\frac{1}{4}$in (57mm) wide, while the risers should be slightly smaller, measuring $\frac{5}{8}$in (16mm) deep by $2\frac{1}{8}$in (54mm). Cut them in $\frac{1}{16}$in (1.5mm) wood. Mahogany or obeche are more attractive than ply.

Stringers can be bought or make your own from the pattern

3 You will find it easier if you make a jig from wood to support the two stringers and keep them parallel. The outside faces of the stringers should be fractionally less than $2\frac{1}{4}$in (57mm) apart. Stick the risers so they sit neatly on the stringers. Glue the treads beyond the risers so that they protrude just a fraction over the front and to one side of the stringer so you have a flat edge to butt against the room wall. You can buy strips of stair nosing to finish off the front edges neatly.

4 Glue a full-length backing to your stairs longer than the staircase. Lightly sand the front and side to take away sharp corners.

A mock hallway is of great assistance when making a staircase

FINISHING THE STAIRCASE

Make yourself a mock hallway from a stiff cardboard box. All you need are two walls and a floor. Mark a line on the rear narrow wall that corresponds to your ceiling height. Cut a slit on and below the line so that you can slide the ¹⁄₁₆in (1.5mm) staircase backing and the top stair tread through it.

Move your stairs back and forth until the treads are horizontal which will give an angle of around 45 degrees. The top tread will be stuck to the underside of your ceiling so, allowing for this, add an extra tread if necessary or take one off if you have too many. When you are satisfied that the staircase is level, make a line below the bottom tread. Glue strips of obeche to the sides of your stairs to cover the rough edges and to give a skirting-board effect.

In real life the spindles sit on the skirting which is usually much thicker. In practice for miniatures you will find it simpler to glue them in the angles between the treads, risers and outer skirting. It may not be authentic but this approach is much easier

Add spindles, top triangle ply and handrail while in the box

and the finished piece is less likely to be damaged. Glue them to the side that will not be attached to the room wall. You also have to taper them as you climb nearer to the ceiling. Glue a triangular piece of ply, cut to shape, near the top at ceiling height. With an enclosed staircase spindles are not needed. A boxed upper stairwell can be used to make a bedroom cupboard.

You will need newel posts (slightly taller than the spindles) for the top and bottom of the stairs; these can be bought or they can be carved out of stripwood.

TIP You should not place the top of your stairs too far to the rear of your hall because you need an area where people can step off and turn to walk along the upper landing. The room doorway and staircase will take up around 12in (305mm) of your room, which is why you need a room depth of at least 15in (380mm). If you do not have this depth, here is an example of when it is sensible to use the solid block type so you can adjust at will.

You will need a room depth of 15in (380mm) for a straight staircase, door and landing space

Another method is to build them from square wood, dowel and beads. To make them stronger, drill holes through the component parts and force a length of brass rod through them.

It is possible to buy ready-made handrails or again you can make one yourself. Cord glued to the top of each spindle, stiffened with paint or glue, is cheap and simple. Alternatively, wood, brass or plastic channelling is available from most hobby shops.

You will need to have a banister round the stairwell on the upper landing. Cut a strip of wood to fit between the newel posts and stick the spindles (equally spaced) or solid panel to it and glue it in position. Never fix landing rails permanently because

A boxed upper stairwell is useful for adding a bedroom cupboard

With an enclosed staircase spindles are not needed

they get knocked every time you put your hand inside to clean or adjust the furniture.

Upholstery material or braiding makes good carpetting and is best glued with a spirit glue. Stair rods can be cut from brass rod.

Right: Landing rails are best left freestanding as they are liable to break when adjusting furniture

STAGGERED STAIRS

If your hall is narrow or very shallow then a straight staircase is not practical and you will need to take a different approach. For an authentic touch to a medieval house, hang a door or curtain at the bottom or halfway up the staircase to keep out draughts.

1 Using the triangular wood method (see page 59), first cut off six or seven stairs. Make a square platform the width of a stair and glue this over the top step of your lower half. Now glue the upper half at right angles to the side of the platform. You can use your cardboard room for this, but lay it on its side for support so you are working side on to the staircase.

2 When the glue has dried, stand the staircase in your house and make sure the treads are flat. Now cut the upper level so the top step is glued under the landing floor.

A staggered staircase is basically two sections with a platform between them

TIP If you want the stairs to double back because the hall is too narrow, make your platform the width of two stairs, remembering to allow a little extra for the skirting and banisters. It may be easier to make the platform the full width of your hall so the upper half of the stairs can fit against the wall.

If the hall is very narrow, the upper flight can double back parallel with the lower section

A SPIRAL STAIRCASE

Spiral stairs were created in the eighteenth and nineteenth centuries. Such stairs are more often found in servants' quarters, leading to attics, or in castle turrets. My first attempts were not entirely successful, so I decided to try a simpler approach for this book. White ³⁄₃₂in (2.5mm) obeche wood is ideal for the job.

1 Cut 12 or 13 stair treads, 3in (75mm) x 1¼in (32mm). Mark off a line 2¼in (57mm) from one end and also a hole positioned just outside this line and towards one edge. The surplus length of tread is so the wood doesn't split while drilling.

2 Stack the treads in two piles, holding them together with double-sided tape. Now drill a hole right through using a drill bit to the diameter of your dowelling centre pole. Take the top tread of the first pile and tape it to the second pile to use as a guide. This measure will prevent the hole slipping off centre when drilling. Now cut off the surplus behind the hole.

3 Draw a diagonal line from the outer edge to the inner side of the hole and cut through the entire pile. You should now have about 13 stairs, each a sort of wedge shape.

4 Next cut the risers. You need to make them fractionally smaller to allow for the step to overhang. Mine are 2³⁄₁₆in (55mm) x ⅝in (16mm).

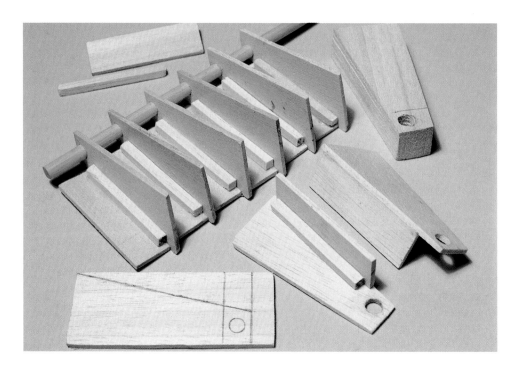

Various steps in making a spiral staircase

5 Glue each riser to the angled edge of the tread, strengthening it with a piece of stripwood underneath. Note the risers stop short of your centre pole. Sand the join and lightly round the front and side of the treads.

6 Mark your dowelling to the height of the room. Allow a little extra to fit in a lower floor hole, or to rise above the ceiling to form a newel post. Whatever you choose, mark the exact length required between the floors and thread your stairs on to it, laying them flat to start with. You can now see whether you have the right number of stairs and whether you are going to have one stair a fraction over or under. You may have to trim your risers or remake one or two of the less obtrusive stairs a fraction higher. This is the stage when you see if you have the right twist.

7 Glue each stair to the next on the straight edge of the tread below it and with a piece of stripwood behind for strength. You must keep every hole in line – use the dowelling as a guide.

8 When you have added your spindles to the outer edge (I used half-round stripwood), adding a curved handrail is tricky. Your easiest option may be to make it from painted cord – well glued to make it stiff before painting.

The size of the treads and risers determines the twist for access up and down stairs

TIP
Using my measurements you may find the top stair does not twist round to the angle you require on the upper landing. If this is the case you will need to remake each tread deeper, or perhaps just the bottom two or three, to give you the right curve.

CHAPTER SIX

EXTERIORS

MANY ENTHUSIASTS are more interested in the interior decoration and furnishing of the house than in its external appearance. However, if you remember that the first impression visitors will receive is of the house in a closed situation, you will see that the outside deserves due consideration. It is often the exterior of the dolls' house that causes most difficulty when decorating but this need not be the case if you follow a few helpful suggestions and gain a little know-how. There are always simple ways of doing what looks difficult and many alternatives to buying expensive features.

WINDOWS

Windows and doors are the most frequently changed feature of a house according to what fashion dictates. You may want your dolls' house to be, say, seventeenth century outside but nineteenth century inside and your windows could reflect this.

In medieval times windows were just open slats with shutters. Glass was in use in the grandest mansions by the mid-sixteenth century but it was very expensive so the panes were small and thick, linked by lead strips. The earliest glass windows were all fixed. When opening casements became practical they were strengthened by iron surrounds. Over the centuries the panes became larger and the glazing bars thinner. From the 1830s glass had become mass produced so it was possible to have larger panes and wooden frames, and sash windows came into fashion.

I usually start by making the windows. This is because I have noticed that craftspeople selling ready-built whitewood houses often put in glazing bars that are far too thick and in such a position that they do not leave room for the glazing. So if you are making your own house or a kit, leave the window holes blank; if the bars are already in place but are not in scale or will prove difficult to glaze, simply cut them out.

Leaded glass can be simulated by scoring Perspex

What should you choose for the glass? Although stiff acrylic sheet is frequently used, I do not like it. The acrylic scratches quite easily and becomes discoloured, and cracked over time. Sheet Perspex, as thin as you can buy, is far superior even if it is more trouble to cut. Any good hardware store, hobby shop, timber merchant or glazier will stock small sheets, and offcuts will cost very little.

Miniaturists may be limited to what they can buy in ready-made windows and they are expensive. My thatched cottage was another abandoned shell which came with these bought windows not yet fitted. Looking at them I realized they were quite simple to make and you can create any size you want.

Buying windows for the whole house is expensive when they are so easy to make to any size or style

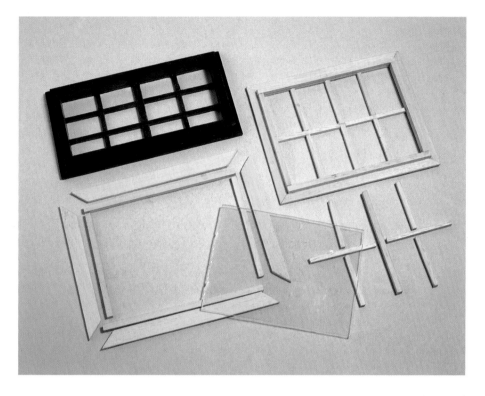

All you need are two thicknesses of square stripwood and one thin flat stripwood plus Perspex

WINDOWS TYPE 1

1 Make a template with card in the same manner as you did for the door. Now take stripwood the same thickness as the wood used for the outside walls. I always use ¼in (6mm) but if your walls are ⅜in (9mm) then use this thickness.

2 Make a frame to sit inside the window hole which can be slid in and out as a close fit. To this frame glue flat stripwood wider than the frame to form the architrave on the outside wall. The corners need to be mitred to 45 degrees.

3 Turn the window over and glue in the glazing bars flush with the architrave. These should be thinner than the frame wood to allow the glass to be inserted on the inside. Use any pattern you wish.

4 Make a frame of narrow stripwood to fit round the glass and hold it in place. Add the inside architraves so they just cover the join between the window frame and the room wall.

TIP You can buy ready-made opening sash windows but they have a drawback. They are so precision-made that they do not allow for the thickness of paint so staining is the only option.

For the frame glue vertical bars first. For the glazing-bars it's horizontal first

WINDOWS TYPE 2

The windows I usually make are very simple, and even if they are a little time-consuming to build they are well worth the effort.

1 Make a card template of your window hole and use this to cut out the Perspex. I use a vibratory saw with a No.7 blade which avoids splintering. If you find the Perspex splinters when you are cutting, cover it with sticky tape on both sides and then cut. If you are using an extra thin Perspex, use a craft

TIP If you find it difficult to cut on a straight line, the Perspex can be shaved by scraping a craft blade over the edge until it is a comfortable fit in the window hole. Sandpaper can also be used to rub down any curves or bumps.

knife. Check that the Perspex fits the window hole really well.

2 Take lengths of narrow stripwood about $\frac{1}{16}$in (1.5mm) thick and paint or stain it on both sides.

3 Run glue right round the window hole. UHU spirit glue tends to smear over the glass, so use Tacky Glue or any water-based glue that dries clear and wipes off easily.

4 Slide the Perspex into the hole to sit in the middle of the house wood and leave to set but not harden.

5 Cut the painted stripwood to fit down each side of the window and glue it over the glazing, tight against the wall. Now cut and glue in the crossbars, top and bottom. Repeat this on the other side of the window making sure it is flush with the outer and inner walls. You can use UHU spirit glue here but not too thickly. The best way is to use your finger so you

can get an even smear along the length and the edge that will bind it to the wall. Tweezers are also useful at this point.

6 Glue glazing bars in the same manner over the Perspex in the pattern you have chosen. Put in the two horizontal bars first and then the vertical. Again, your finger will make sure there is not too much glue and that it does not run over the edge.

STYRENE STRIPS

Model railway and some hobby shops sell styrene strips in all thicknesses and widths. This can be expensive if you have a lot of windows but it is the only material you can use if you have curved windows. You can stretch and curve it with your fingers to fit round the window. I used this on the station shown. For the castle I used 1mm square styrene strips. As there were so many bars I used Tacky Glue instead of UHU spirit glue, as this was less messy. It is a case of trial and error until you find what is easiest.

TIP Lighter fuel or even worn sandpaper will rub glue from your finger. If you do get glue on the Perspex do not try to rub it off while it is still wet. When it is partially dry you can roll it with a sliver of soft stripwood. Don't rub too hard or you will scratch the Perspex and if you try while it is fresh then you will make matters worse by causing it to smear permanently.

Square styrene strips painted grey look more like leaded glazing

Narrow styrene strips can be stretched to fit round curves

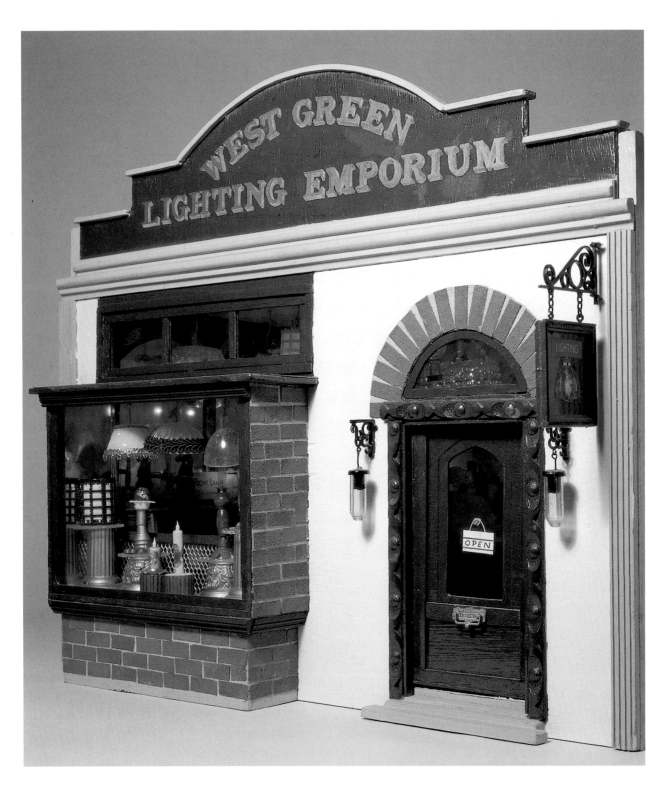

Pared down to its basics, this bay window is no more than a box with a window in it, glued to the wall

Different layers of framing gives the impression of thick walls

For a three-window bay start with the base and roof

WINDOWS TYPE 3

To simulate thick castle walls I took advantage of the kit's ⅜in (9mm) wood. I cut the arched window from thinner wood, added a second square frame, leaving another step on the original wood. A little way in from the edge I glued a raised beading. Chunky glazing bars complete the illusion.

WINDOWS TYPE 4

Bay windows add something special to a house and are not really difficult to make.

The square one-window bay is no more than a box with a window in it which is then glued to the wall. Make the box sides to fit inside the wall's window hole.

The bay with three windows is best made by starting with the base and roof and making three separate windows in their own frames which can then be glued together between the top and bottom. Don't forget to allow room for the architraves between the panes.

The rounded bay is not quite so easy but is still possible.

1 Start with two semicircles of wood which protrude no more than ¾in (19mm) at its widest point otherwise you won't be able to bend the Perspex.

2 For the glazing bars make a template in card using the top or base as a pattern. Use this to cut three pieces of obeche wood – available in long lengths measuring 3in (75mm) wide. The thickness is variable but I suggest about ¼in (6mm.) Glue two of the bars to the top and base. Add uprights to each side so you have a firm frame to which you can glue the third bar across the centre. It isn't too difficult now to add vertical bars between the three horizontal bars. The whole window is now ready to glue to the outside of the window hole.

3 Adding the Perspex can be a problem if it is too thick. You need to bend it round so it is in contact with the glazing bars. Hold it in place with a windowsill cut to that curve. You will need another sill for the ceiling. To hold the Perspex more firmly, add inside uprights down each side.

A rounded bay on a really old house or shop gives it an antiquated appeal

WINDOWS TYPE 5

Leaded windows were first made in order to hold glass. Initially glass was very expensive so house builders could only use small panes with leading in between.

Although experts can make the real thing in miniature, there are simpler ways. A really easy way is to buy acrylic sheets with ready painted black lines and fix it to the Perspex. However over time the acrylic will shrink, stretch or discolour.

My method is to scribe the lines on the Perspex and smear black emulsion paint all over. Clean it off while still wet, being careful not to remove the paint from the scoring.

Another way is to cut fine strips of black paper and glue them to the window. Alternatively you can buy self-adhesive black strips. There are also tubes of liquid paint but these require a steady hand.

Leaded panes can be made by scoring the Perspex with a diamond pattern then filling with black emulsion paint

BOTTLE GLASS

The base of many soft drink bottles has a round disc created by the break-off point in manufacture. Cut out this disc and make a corresponding hole in your Perspex windowpane. Glue discs into the windowpanes in a random pattern.

The base of plastic drink bottles make realistic bottle glass

STAINED GLASS

Again the experts know how to make stained glass to perfection. It is possible to buy lead strip which is thinner than that for our own home windows. Some people cut the normal lead into fine strips but the result can look rather bulky.

I use a model railway lining pen. This is best described as a pelican beak with a well to hold the paint and a screw mechanism which holds the gap to your chosen width.

1 Take a card and mark the area of the window. If you are not an artist, trace a picture and transfer it to the card.

2 Place the Perspex on top of the design and cut to size. You can follow the lines with the lining pen. I find battleship-grey Humbrol an ideal paint to use.

3 Use a glass paint to fill in the coloured areas between the 'lead'.

Paint the outlines with a lining pen

Stained glass for houses became popular during Victorian times

TIP Glass paint is available from hobby and art-supply shops in a wide range of colours. When filling in the coloured areas, use plenty of paint in one go as you can drag the surplus to one corner and lift it out with the brush. If you try to give your stained glass a second coat you will end up with a blotchy picture because the second melts the first. Make sure you paint right up to the lead without leaving any clear areas showing.

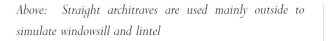

Above: Straight architraves are used mainly outside to simulate windowsill and lintel

Right: Architraves inside are mitred, though the bottom horizontal can be straight across to give it a windowsill

ARCHITRAVES

Choose the width of stripwood you need and paint it before cutting. There are two ways of applying the architraves – one simple, one needing a mitre.

Take the simple way first, the one which is best for using around some types of doors and also for the outside of windows. Cut two lengths to fit exactly from top to bottom of the window hole. Cut away a sliver of wallpaper all round the window so that it will not show as a rough edge. Glue the vertical architraves down the sides, positioning them to be a fraction over the join where the frame meets the wall. Now cut the cross pieces top and bottom of the window, wider than the window and beyond the vertical architraves. This looks like a lintel and windowsill. If you want a real windowsill, use a thicker piece of stripwood and glue it along the edge so it protrudes from the window. You may have to add a bracket or square strip underneath to support the sill.

Professional architraves are mitred. At the corners of the surround you cut the stripwood at 45 degrees. Use the columns of text of a newspaper to ensure your corners meet at right angles (see page 51).

TIP Wherever you join wood there will be a line or even a minute gap. Go round every glazing bar and architrave and apply a smear of thin plaster filler. You will probably have to repaint these small areas. A worn artist's brush with a few hairs is ideal for this job.

Right: Fill in the joint gaps with a thin plaster filler

Repaint the small areas which have been filled

CASEMENT WINDOWS

Casement windows are made in the same way as for pinned doors (see page 49). The sill has to be glued in the window hole after inserting the pin just as you do for the doorstep.

Dressmaker's pins are used as hinges to create an opening casement

PAINTING

The vast majority of miniaturists merely paint the outside of their house. However, you can transform a simple dolls' house into a realistic model with more detailed decoration. A simply painted house is fine for children but even they like to see more realism and brick paper can help achieve this very easily.

If you are painting all or part of the outside never use gloss paint. It makes the building look out of scale. Vinyl silk emulsion is the best and now some traders are offering small sample pots which are ideal for miniaturists. You can also buy sample tins of sanded paint if you want a rough texture. If you use gloss, say for the window surrounds, then rub it down with a very fine wire wool. Wire wool is also excellent for giving a smooth surface between coats. It will also remove any runs that have appeared. Several thin coats instead of one thick one will avoid the tendency to form runs.

PLASTER RENDERING

Plaster rendering is often used on country cottages or as infill for timber houses. Using the real thing is messy and it is not easy to give a rough finish that is truly in the 1:12 scale. There are so many embossed wallpapers available today that you are sure to find one that is more realistic. Paint the paper with white emulsion and cut it to fit the areas where rendering is needed. Glue it in position using a diluted wood glue.

It isn't easy to use plaster filler without making a mess and yet keeping it in scale

Embossed paper is cleaner to use than plaster

Pargeting was a fashion in the sixteenth and seventeenth centuries. This was an art form in which plasterwork was incised with ornamental patterns. For the dolls' house you can use filigree jewellery pieces glued to the walls and painted over with white emulsion. On the kit house I have used what was the surround for the original circular window with plastic date numbers inside.

Embossed paper used in the earth closet has mildew and cobwebs added. The same paper on the roof forms roofing felt (tarred paper)

Left: Pargeting can be as simple as a date or an elaborate picture carving

WEATHERBOARDING

Weatherboarding came into fashion in the late eighteenth to mid-nineteenth centuries, though it was in use from 1690. It is more common in the south-east of England and even more widely seen in America. It was first devised to make certain walls waterproof if they were exposed to the prevailing bad weather. It also became popular when the house owner wanted to hide an unfashionable façade.

When you apply weatherboarding to a house, you will have to cut round windows or doors to fit it. If the colour you want to paint it is different to the colour of your window and door frames, paint the contact points of the weatherboarding before gluing it in position. If you are staining the wood, do this before gluing.

1 Cut ¹⁄₁₆in (1.5mm) ply into long strips. Starting at the bottom of the wall, glue your first strip. Use a spirit glue as opposed to a water-based adhesive or you will find that the planks warp as they dry.

2 Gradually glue one strip above the other, overlapping each lower strip by just a fraction. At the top you may have to cut a narrower strip to finish.

Weatherboarding was used to protect walls or to hide an unfashionable façade

If there is a colour contrast where the planks fit round windows then paint contact points before gluing

Below: Weatherboarding on old barns is usually stained. Do this before gluing

STONE RENDERING

Stone rendering was another way to make walls weatherproof. You see it most often in areas where flint is plentiful, such as Norfolk and counties of south-east England. Builders would use whatever material was available locally. Stone rendering was also used on original timber houses when their wattle and daub began to wear. Owners used to fill the gaps with rubble which is what I have implied on the thatched cottage (see below). Brick infill was not used until bricks were mass produced and therefore cheap.

This cottage has been made to simulate wear over the centuries

When I decided to make a flint house I searched for suitable material. Using crushed real flint was dangerous because of its sharp edges. People love to touch the walls and I could not risk accidents. In my search I found some aquarium gravel that had a smooth surface – it was not perfect but was practical. The bags had all sizes of pebbles which I sorted into three grades. On one wall I used the middle size but it didn't look in scale so thereafter I used the smallest stones. (The larger ones have since come in useful for road cobbles.) The stones also had a wide variety of colours and were the nearest I could find to resemble flint which normally has all shades of grey, white and black with sandstone mixed in.

All flint walls must have a solid surround of wood or brick. This means around windows and doors and to divide large areas of flint. Corners are usually strengthened with brick coigning. Another common style is alternating horizontal stripes. The pattern of bricks to flint is entirely up to you.

I usually use quality birch ply for my houses but as this building was going to be well covered I bought the cheaper ply.

Flint walls must have a solid surround of wood or brick. The pattern of brick to flint is a matter of choice

1 Cut out a pattern in ⅛in (3mm) MDF board to fit over the walls where you intend having brick; glue it on to the walls. Paint it a mortar colour.

2 Mix Tetrion plaster with Unibond glue and a little water to form a reasonably malleable paste and spread it in one area of your prepared wall.

3 Tip a handful of stones into the paste and press and push them around to form a single layer which fills the designated area. Try not to dirty the top of the stones and have a wet cloth handy to wipe paste from what will be the bricked area.

4 Shake off the surplus stones when the paste has partially set. You will see small gaps appear which can be filled with individual stones of the appropriate size and shape to give an overall covering – tweezers are a useful tool here. Be careful to scrape off unwanted paste before it dries completely as it sets rock hard.

5 Now you need to brick the surrounds (see section to follow).

Step-by-step method for making a flint wall

TIP Unibond is a white PVA all-purpose glue, stronger than wood glue for adhering the smooth stones to the wall. The depth of paste should be enough to firmly embed the stones.

BRICK-MAKING

Bricks have been used since Roman times and varied in size over the centuries

The size of bricks has varied over the centuries. Roman bricks were thin and hand made. After the Romans left Britain these bricks were often reused in later buildings. Bricks were again popular in the thirteenth to fifteenth centuries. By the mid-sixteenth century they were thicker, and in the seventeenth century elaborate brickwork was introduced. In the Georgian period the taste was for grey, brown, buff and yellow. Bricks were used as dressing and quoins, again to cover unfashionable frontages.

Loose dolls'-house bricks can be bought in packets but they are very expensive. These are usually made of resin and have a smooth surface, making them look rather unrealistic. You can buy sheets of bricks which feel rough but again are expensive, plus these sheets have to be cut and joined and the joins are not always easy to hide. Another unfavourable feature is that commercial bricks tend to be a uniform red whereas real bricks come out from firing in a variety of shades.

Over the years I have experimented with many ideas for making bricks - thin ply (not worth trying) plaster, sand and even real bricks ground to a powder. Eventually I pioneered a method using sheets of sandpaper which proved successful and very cheap. I have used these sandpaper bricks for a variety of other uses including fireplaces, a forge, a coal bin and a clothes boiler.

To carry out this technique, you will need a safe cutting board (see below) to protect your fingers. For the bricks I use F2 grade sandpaper which has a brick-like feel, is flexible and sticks firmly to the painted mortar surface. The whole procedure is safe and effective.

1 Use Blu-Tack to secure the sheet to the work surface because if you use your finger to hold it the paint will come off with the sand. Paint the sheet in a brick-red colour using matt emulsion. Before it is dry smear the surface with other mixtures of colours and smudge or stipple them over the base colour to give a random mottled effect. Leave to dry and then you are ready to cut.

2 Butt the sheet against the board edge. Butt your steel ruler against the mini blocks, which should be

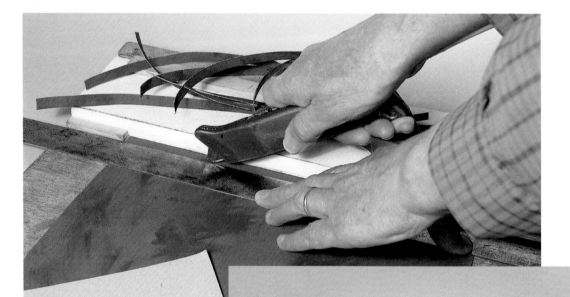

Cutting even strips is simple and safe with a home-made cutting board

CUTTING BOARD

This consists of a board of any thickness but it must be at least 12in (305mm) wide. To the rear of this glue or screw a piece of thicker wood, like a step, preferably covered with laminate to give a regular surface. Now cut two short blocks of wood ¼in (6mm) wide and stick one to each end of your board and against the back step using double-sided tape. These blocks can be changed for other sizes for, say, paving stones. You will also need a craft knife and a wide steel ruler. To the back of the upper board I have glued/screwed two strips of MDF. One is a fraction over ¾in (19mm) deep and behind that there is another strip slightly thicker so it forms a buffer.

identical and spaced apart so the metal will just rest against them at either end. Cut on the inside between the blocks and remove the strip. Push the sandpaper up against the board edge and repeat until you have cut all the sheet into strips.

3 To chop the strips into bricks, turn the board round to use the two extra wood pieces at the back. Press the end of a strip up against the higher step, bend it over the edge of the board to form a crease and cut along this line. Leave some long strips for the part bricks. You should now have individual bricks ¾in (19mm) long and ¼in (6mm) deep.

Use the guide at the rear of your cutting board to chop the strips into bricks

4 Mix and pick the bricks up at random as you glue them to the wall to give an authentic mottled brick effect. I use UHU spirit glue as any overflow dries clear. Keep going back over the wall to press down the bricks in case any are lifting. Touch up the edges with paint round any corners where the sandpaper shows. You can also repaint odd bricks if the colour distribution is not quite right or you need to add weathering. (Bricking is a long tedious job but the effect is well worth the effort. I relieve the boredom by doing one wall at a time with something more interesting in between.)

Picking up your bricks at random will give you a more realistic colour variation

Flemish

English

BRICK BONDS

There are four basic patterns of laying brick bonds to choose from

Stretcher

Header

HERRINGBONE

Herringbone is an attractive pattern used on older buildings. It took me all of the inside of my market hall to work out how the pattern evolved! I had also covered half the building outside before I found an easier method. The problem was that when gluing the bricks direct to the painted surface I was left with odd triangles round the edges which were often very small. In making the sample board I realized that it was far easier to paint the wallpaper with the rendering colour and mark out an area corresponding to the panel I needed to fill. Glue your bricks over this area, extending them beyond the pencil lines where they fall. You can now cut through the bricks and paper to fit your panel exactly and the whole area is covered without those irritating gaps. Use a wood glue to attach them to the building.

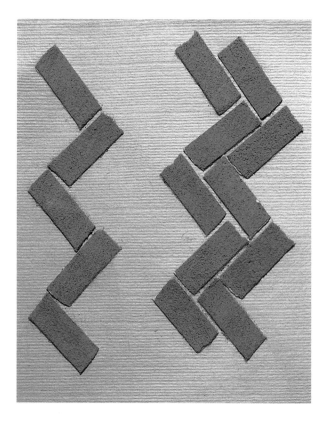

Start with a simple row then the pattern builds up from that

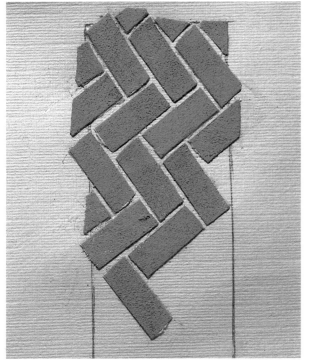

Above: Roughly mark out the panel area and glue the bricks over this

Above right: Cut the panel to size and glue it in the designated area

Right: Tichfield Market Hall is a model of the original now the centrepiece at the open air museum in West Sussex. I added the market street scene for extra interest

STONE WALLING

Stone bricks for a castle, church or hill cottage are similar to making roof tiles (see page 107). You can make the paper stones as with the red bricks and glue them direct. This isn't quite so effective and creates a flatter look. To cut down the weight I used paper stones on the inside of the tower but I still prefer the plywood bricks.

I used grey bricks but yellow sandstone would be just as effective

1 Paint a large irregular swirling pattern of embossed wallpaper with various shades of grey or sandstone. Use a different shade for each sheet, again smeared with different shades.

2 Make bricks from ¹⁄₁₆in (1.5mm) ply or card by first cutting it into strips and then into individual bricks. Sand all the edges and glue them to the reverse side of your painted sheets. When dry they can be cut round with a craft knife and you have a pile of stone bricks.

3 Mix up the bricks and pick them up at random and glue them to the walls to create the desired mottled effect, leaving a minute gap between each stone. Use impact glue while still wet. This gives you time to move them for lining up the rows but keep going over them to press them down until the glue has set.

4 The rendering is made from plaster filler dyed with a little black and yellow colouring (I used powder paint).

Glue wood bricks to the underside of embossed paper, painted in various shades of grey

TIP A warning here, the filler on matt paper is hard to remove so paint the wall with a coat of thin varnish (diluted wood glue) then the surplus filler can be washed off.

WALL TILES

Hung tiles is a common form of weather protection, usually on the upper half

Wall hung tiles, usually on the upper half, is another form of wall protection very common in Surrey and Sussex in the UK. They may be square, diamond-shaped or scalloped. Often there is a mixture of styles arranged in a variety of patterns.

The straight or diamond tiles are first cut in $\frac{1}{16}$in (1.5mm) ply, glued to the back of brick-painted sandpaper and cut round. Paint the ply edges before cutting; see roof tiling. When glued to the wall the whitewood shows badly if you don't and

it's harder to paint *in situ* especially between the fine gaps.

Square or diamond tiles are no problem and neither are the scallops when you know the secret. You can buy bags of smooth scallops, but these are expensive, or the ridged cedar-wood type which are irregular in thickness and harder to glue and paint. The best idea is to buy cheap tongue depressors from your chemist. From each of these you will obtain two scallops and two straights.

BLACK AND WHITE TIMBER FRAMING

Left: The Tudor period with its black and white timber framing is always popular with dolls' house enthusiasts

Below: This chemist with upper sculpture gallery is merely two boxes stacked (for easy transport to exhibitions). The outside steps are made stone-like by pressing powdered sawdust into glue

The very first timber houses had large framing with panels 6ft (183cm) square with diagonal bracing, arched, herringbone or cross-shaped. From the mid-fifteenth century, smaller framing was introduced, being about 2 to 3ft (61 to 91cm). Close-set framing dates from the 1500s and was popular in well-wooded areas. The more timber used the higher the cost of building so close-set framing showed wealth. By the seventeenth century large framing was enhanced by elaborate ornamental pattern. Then Britain entered a period where there was an acute shortage of oak as it was being used to make ships. Instead, lighter brick-built houses appeared or rough timber was covered with plaster, tiles or weatherboarding.

The painted black and white effect came into fashion with the Victorians. Originally the oak was seasoned and left as a natural wood. Surprisingly, the timber on some early houses was painted red and examples can still be found in France and Germany. There are also regional patterns for the timber framing throughout Britain.

I love this architectural style, so I make many houses using it. For my timber framing I use lengths of obeche wood. It comes in a variety of thicknesses

Make a card template of the curved beams before cutting them in wood

and is always 3in (75mm) wide. For the curved braces I first make a card template to fit the radius or angle needed. The infill is white-painted embossed wallpaper cut to fit tightly in each section. In real life the curved braces originated from one tree cut down the centre so they had a matching pair.

This building can be separated into three sections. The centre house has a restaurant downstairs and a museum displaying charcoal burning and lead smelting upstairs. To give it more interest I added a kitchen on the right and an arcade on the left. The timber has been stained rather than painted black

CHAPTER SEVEN

ROOFING

For this station roof I used left over imitation brick tiles used in real houses, using the cutting board with larger blocks for the right size

I USE SEVERAL DIFFERENT TYPES OF ROOFING on my houses, all comparatively simple but nevertheless effective. Wood, card, vinyl and hay can all be used in a variety of ways to simulate most roofing materials.

SLATES

Slate has been quarried since Roman times but before the nineteenth century it was only used locally in Wales. When railways became established and the slate could be transported with ease, it was used extensively throughout Britain.

- The easiest method of making imitation slates for dolls' houses is to cut them from cereal boxes.

- A more effective way is to buy price tag labels – the ones with a curved end and a hole to hold the string. These can be used either way down according to whether you want a scalloped or plain tile. The scalloped ends make a very effective ridge tile.

Price tag labels can be used either way down. They give an authentic appearance for tiles

• Another easy idea is to cut 1in (25mm) wide strips of $\frac{1}{16}$in (1.5mm) ply slightly longer than the roof, though this isn't important if the house is large. Now draw lines across each strip to the size of your slate, probably at 1in (25mm) intervals. The quickest way is to cut a scrap of wood to this width and use it as a template. Cut along these lines but only for three-quarters of each marker. Starting at the bottom of your roof, glue a length of tiling from one side to the other. The second row is staggered so the grooves alternate all the way to the top. Each row covers the uncut area of the strips. The top row may need to be less deep when you reach the ridge.

• Some kits provide slates (tiles) where the wood is no thicker than veneer. Do not try to stick these with a water-based glue as they will warp in all directions.

Above: A template of wood is quicker than using a ruler for marking lines

Right: Each strip is staggered so the tiles alternate

Wood bricks are glued to reverse side of painted sandpaper

- Clay tiles were introduced in Britain as early as 1477. Using my ever-versatile red stippled sandpaper I make the tiles from $\frac{1}{16}$in (1.5mm) ply by first cutting the strips and then chopping then into individual tiles. These will have to be sanded and then glued to the reverse side of the sandpaper. Paint the edges before cutting them from the sandpaper because, as with the wall tiles, the plain wood shows badly and is difficult to paint *in situ*. Glue them to the roof with impact glue remembering to stagger each row. Fill in the gaps at the gable ends with plaster, then paint.

On an old building, the tiles can chip or slip to age the roof. Neat rows would be more appropriate on a stately home

Use your finger to smear plaster into the gaps at the gable ends

- After the nineteenth century heavy building materials — sandstone, limestone and shale — became popular. These stones were quite large along the eaves and gradually became less deep as they neared the ridge. In Sussex, UK, the heavy quarry stone slabs were used extensively. I needed Horsham quarrystone for my Sussex farmhouse and I could not find anything suitable. I tried all the Anaglypta wallpapers but even the smallest didn't look right. I squashed the bumps with a piece of wood. It still didn't look right until it fell on the floor upside down — and there was my quarrystone! I used this instead of sandpaper and made the tiles in the same way, except that I cut the long strips into graduated sizes, keeping the individual tiles the same width all the way up. To give a feeling of age, I applied random patches of glue to the roof and then sprinkled fine sawdust

Note how heavy stone tiles start large at the eaves and gradually become smaller near the ridge

over it, brushing off any excess when dried, giving the impression of plant life. I also used model railway flock. The moss and lichen were painted *in situ*.

- Ridge tiles are made from right-angle stripwood. This comes in two sizes and also a curved shape. Cut it into 2in (50mm) lengths and glue them over the ridge to cover the top edge of tiles on both sides of the roof.

THATCHING

Thatch has been used since 500 BC. The pitch of thatched roofs is much steeper to ensure rainwater runs off.

Dolls'-house owners find thatch irresistible. The problem is to find a material that lends itself to 1:12 scale. So what is the best material for a realistic effect? And how can it be applied without the notoriously messy glue problem? I have answered both these questions and at exhibitions I am constantly asked how I do it.

Every conceivable material has been used by miniaturists. Some are really awful, such as using fake fur fabric. I have seen a whole doormat used too! Raffia just looks like raffia – its flat strands are too wide and irregular. Corn or wheat stalks have too large a diameter so the roof appears top-heavy and they are not easy to apply either. Unravelled garden string is passable from a distance but rather tweedy in close-up. Plumbers hemp is too fine. Fine basket cane has the right thickness but the wood is polished and expensive and has to be used while damp. Bristle from floor brushes is the most popular. It's cheaper if offcuts are bought direct from a brush factory. However, even when well applied it is the wrong colour and you cannot disguise the fact that it is bristle. Coir is the latest thatch material available.

After years of research I opted for hay. Commercial hay can be extremely dusty, and may contain weeds and even dried manure. If you buy hay that mainly comprises thick stalks, you will find these are slippery and when gluing the inner strands slide out. The best solution is to hand cut tall grass which should then be sun-dried. A whole sackful is needed for each 1:12 dolls' house because there is a lot of wastage.

What better material to use for a tithe barn than natural hay?

Make yourself a narrow channel for a bundle of hay

The most natural-looking thatching job results from copying the professionals. Tie the hay in small bundles using a simple home-made gadget. It is a narrow channel 3in (75mm) long and made of ½in (13mm) square stripwood with a removable PVC cover stapled or attached with Velcro to the baseboard. When the hay is trapped in the channel you have both hands free and a guide to cut each bundle to the same length. Secure one end of the bundle with sticky tape and trim the ends.

TIP Don't use a vacuum cleaner for the hay waste on the floor until you've scraped up the bulk of the grass. It will cause a blockage in your machine.

The clamp leaves your hands free to tie one end and cut the other

GLUING THATCH

The gluing process can be a messy procedure. Non-drip contact adhesive is preferable, if used with care. Cheap disposable vinyl gloves are ideal and one to two pairs should be sufficient to complete a roof. Coat in talcum powder inside and out; this aids in putting the gloves on and helps to repel a build-up of glue on the fingers.

1 Cut 2in (50mm) wide strips of thin cotton material the length of the roof width. Cover your work bench with a sheet of polythene. Use drawing pins to attach a strip to the bench. Glue the upper end of each hay bundle and lay them side by side along the strip, pressing them on. Leave until reasonably set.

On the underside spread glue all over the cotton strip and hay

Trim the edge back to the 3in (75mm) line

2 Turn the thatching strip over and glue the whole of the underside including the material. A screwdriver is useful here to hold the cloth as you glue each bundle. It is easier to realign the thatch at this stage. Hold the strip vertically and trim the edge back to the 3in (75mm) line. Lay along the lower edge of your roof. Slice through the sticky tape now so you can spread the strands more evenly and avoid bulk.

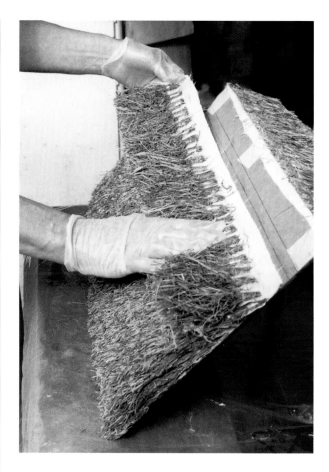

As you continue adding strips don't leave too large a gap between each layer or it looks ridged and thin

TIP This is the messy stage as your spreader will be covered in glued hay. Instead of using a rag, scrape the glue off with the screwdriver on to a sheet of heavier plastic. When dry but not hard peel off the waste so the sheet can be used again. The bulk left on the gloves can be plucked off with tweezers then sprinkle with talcum powder. Lighter fuel or petrol will clean off any minor mess.

Unruly hay can be pasted down with diluted glue

Dry the glue with a hairdryer

3 Dry hay is springy so work diluted Tacky Glue into the upper side of the strip. Dry with a hair dryer and press down. Cut away any uneven strands.

Right: Trim off any uneven strands

Apply adhesive to all but the final layer of thatching left exposed

4 Now the springy hay has been stabilized, spread the layer of thatch with contact adhesive and add the next strip, and so on to the top. Near the ridge the bundles get progressively shorter. Do not make the overlaps between rows too far apart and remember not to apply adhesive on what will be the exposed portion because it will dry as an ugly mass.

5 The ridge is made by first gluing scrap hay to a strip of cartridge paper. Tie thinner, longer bundles and glue over the rough layer but cut off the tied end as soon as you've pressed it into place, and spread the strands evenly. Paint the hay with diluted Tacky Glue.

Use scrap hay as an underlay on the cartridge paper, then add a neat spread of hay on top

Hand sew the crosshatching with crochet thread and glue ridge over the top

6 When dry, trim the edges and hand sew the crosshatching. Glue the ridge down over the upper layers of thatch.

7 Give the thatch a final trim and tidy up the gable ends by adding more hay where necessary.

8 Coat the surface with diluted Tacky Glue as it needs to be smooth so it can be dusted but still looks like thatch. Don't worry if the dried hay still has a green tinge. It bleaches out naturally after a few days in the sun, or a little longer indoors.

After six years searching for realistic thatch, my tithe barn is finally finished

On the barn shown above, I did not include the traditional overhang. To achieve this, a double row of thatch to the bottom layer would have given more pronounced eaves.

The barn was made authentically with rafters so for the thatch I made a removable roof of MDF board to fit snugly over the beams. I thatched it on the workbench outdoors to disperse the glue fumes.

Dowelling pegs inserted into holes in the fixed ridge pole keeps the false roof steady and yet it is still removable

THATCHED COUNTRY COTTAGE

This house had four rooms plus a landing but like most miniaturists I wanted to make use of the loft space. The problems were, how to thatch dormer windows and how to make an opening roof.

Unlike the barn with its open rafters, the cottage roof was solid, though I had cut an opening in the front half. However, I still opted for a secondary removable roof. This was partly because I was experimenting and I could start again if it didn't go as visualized and it would reduce the weight when transporting the house to exhibitions.

Again I used ⅛in (3mm) MDF board for the two halves of the false roof but this time I hinged them at the ridge with a piano hinge. Three holes were drilled just below the hinge on the rear at such an angle that the drill went into the triangular stripwood used for the ridge pole inside the fixed roof. I glued ¼in (6mm) dowelling into holes in the false roof so that when these were slotted into the corresponding holes in the fixed roof, the outer shell didn't move around but was still easy to remove when necessary.

I then made three normal box dormer windows but extended the fronts in ¼in (6mm) ply to give an 'eyebrow' effect. I bricked these fronts on the workbench using my usual method of painted sandpaper (see pages 94–95). The dormers needed a support for the thatch. I used the thin and flexible ⅟₃₂in (0.8mm) ply and pin-tacked it neatly to the upper curves of the 'eyebrows'. You could also use card. The rear end which rested against the roof was quite tricky. The thin ply could be cut and chipped away with scissors until it rested against the roof,

leaving the windows in a vertical position against the sloping roof. It did not matter that the result was a little rough because it would be covered with thatch and beyond the neat box recesses seen from inside. As added support I stuck small blocks of stripwood on the underside of the ply so they also stuck to the roof slope.

I followed the same method of thatching as I did for the barn; it was just a case of laying the strips so they followed the contours and filling in where necessary with odd bundles of hay.

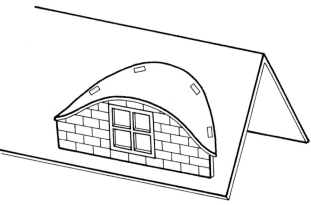

Above: diagram to explain the adding of 'eyebrow' dormer windows on to a thatched roof

The strips of hay were layered on the roof, following the contours round the 'eyebrow' windows

The front was beginning to take shape but on the rear slope I had first to glue and screw the chimneys to the bare board so they corresponded to the inside fireplaces. I also had to consider the front opening roof which created a problem. I had to ensure it didn't fall on the viewers looking in the top rooms. After exploring many possibilities I placed the chimneys precisely so that when the front roof was open it leaned slightly backwards against the stacks. This method avoided the need for support bars, locks, catches or any other additions. The roof swings up and down freely without risk of falling forward. Thatching the roof was quite straightforward, using the same method as for the barn.

The ridge obviously could not be made in one piece and glued over the apex as before. I solved this problem by making the ridge in two halves so the front piece had the cross-hatching rising slightly above the hinge but not so high that it stopped the roof opening fully. The rear half was glued slightly below the hinge. As the house was to be viewed from the front, the split ridge couldn't be seen.

The ridge had to be split into two halves either side of the hinge

That just left the surrounds of the front fixed roof which looked ugly when the thatched roof was open. Painting didn't look right and took away the whole idea of a thatched cottage. Using the cartridge paper as for the ridges, I cut four strips to fit exactly over the surrounds. To these I glued a thin layer of straight lengths of hay. The lower piece was rather deep so I stitched this section only. The strips were then glued round the opening and painted with diluted Tacky Glue to prevent the hay flaking off with constant use.

Thatching on the original roof surround gives a more authentic appearance when the roof is open

CHIMNEYS

These should follow the internal flues right up to the roof. If you want chimney pots, then make one for each fire. A cheap and easy way is to make them with dowelling, giving a shaped top created with dressmaker's elastic. Chimney pots are vulnerable so I suggest you make them removable by inserting a brass rod in the base.

Cement rendering was simulated by pressing sieved sawdust powder into glue

One chimney pot is needed for each fire in the house

An outside chimney flue forms part of the chimney

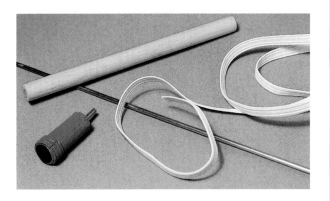

Dressmaker's elastic or ribbon on dowelling can give a shaped top

CHAPTER EIGHT

BALCONIES, VERANDAHS
AND WINDOW-BOXES

AFTER EIGHT MINTS USED TO HAVE metal trays to stand on the table. When the company made the chocolate boxes larger, these trays became obsolete and can now be picked up on market stalls for a few pence. This set me looking for other metal filigree containers as I could see their potential.

Fancy metal boxes and trays can be made into many dolls' house creations

My next find was a fancy tissue-box holder. The box was fairly deep and ideal for a high balcony on the pebble house (see opposite), and the shallower lid would make front railings on the verandah. These boxes usually have a mesh base which is easily cut away with tin snips. Snip down one side by the join and hammer it into one continuous strip. Repeat with the lid.

1 For the verandah cut two lengths of the lid to fit between the posts and either side of the front door.

2 Turn the long lower edge over just a fraction with pliers to give a neat edge and a base to sit on the floor of the walkway. This can be glued and screwed for security.

3 From the leftovers there should be strips to glue under the roof canopy.

The lid of the tissue box was used for the verandah

CHOPSTICKS

Chopsticks make useful posts especially if they have square ends. The dowelling end has many other uses. Glue lengths of the square end behind the metal to give the fence a firmer contact with the tall support posts. Plastic takeaway finger forks with fancy tops can be used for decoration.

1 For the balcony floor screw the wood from the inside of the front opening door.

2 Take your length of the tissue-box base and, as before, bend over the bottom to give a neat edge. Now bend the corners to fit across the front and round the sides of the floor and snip away the surplus.

3 As with the verandah, glue and screw to the balcony floor.

The balcony was made from the fancy metal tissue-box holder

WINDOW-BOXES

An After Eight tray is used here. The round metal handle and feet are solid and you will need a small hacksaw to cut through them. The fancy walls are a softer metal and can be cut with tin snips. I have also made crowns, a medieval chandelier, a fire-back and garden furniture from these metal boxes.

1 Cut a front and two sides with tabs at either end of each piece which are bent inwards. These tabs help to weld the three pieces round the corners.

2 Make a thin wooden box to fit snugly inside the metal frame.

3 For earth, used and dried tea leaves – loose leaf, not tea bags – are a realistic scale. Mix the leaves with glue and fill your box. I usually buy fish tank plants or those used by fishmongers or butchers to separate trays. Plastic flowers are easily dusted or washed.

Cloth flowers are often sold in cake making shops. If you are clever you can make your own. I advise you to drill holes in the 'earth' so the plants can be slotted in and out which makes for easier exchange or cleaning.

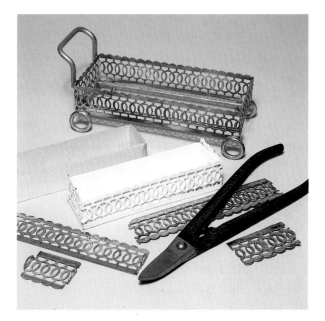

An After Eight chocolate tray, now obsolete, was used to make the window box frame

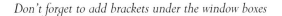

Don't forget to add brackets under the window boxes

CHAPTER NINE

GARDENS – HEDGES, TOPIARY, FENCES AND GATES

A stately home has a neat and formal garden

EVERYONE LOVES A GARDEN so it is a popular subject for the miniaturist. Even dolls' houses are often given a small attached garden which is enclosed by a fence, hedge or wall. For hedges I've used Christmas tree spikes by drilling holes in the baseboard and planting them in a row in the 'earth' as on the station.

Even a farmhouse had its cottage garden and roses round the porch

Yew hedges and topiary are essential for the gardens we associate with stately homes. Polystyrene packing is readily available in various thicknesses but it is very prone to crumbling. A special battery, or mains-operated, cutter can be bought for this material which has a thin heated blade which slices through polystyrene to give a clean surface. I use a vibrating scrollsaw, but a fine-toothed blade on a hand fretsaw is a cheaper alternative.

Country stations were proud of their gardens, often in competition with each other

YEW HEDGE

1 Draw your pattern on the sheet of polystyrene and cut out your hedge. Any holes or chipped edges can be filled with plaster. To strengthen the surface cover the whole area with thin cotton material. This includes top, sides and ends. Use either PVA wood or all purpose Tacky Glue. When dry the hedge will be sturdy and chip proof. If you want to join lengths together at right angles then do this now. This will make for neater corners.

2 Cover your hedge with leaves. Model railway track material is either too powdery or too flocky and does not give the ideal neatly cut yew hedge for a stately home. Instead use tea leaves that have been brewed then dried. Spread your hedge with a generous layer of PVA or Tacky Glue and press the dried tea leaves into it. Leave to harden before you shake off the surplus. Small gaps are of no consequence but if there are bare patches, re-glue and add more leaves.

3 Painting with a brush is rather messy and is apt to rub off the leaves. Car spray paint is a much better option. Here two coats of a forest green with a quick spray of a lighter shade over the top produced a two-tone effect which looked very natural.

Three stages in making the yew hedge

TOPIARY

Yew hedges are essential features of formal gardens

For the topiary birds use the same method. Cut the shape from polystyrene, cover with fabric and then add tea leaves and paint.

The topiary tree is made by cutting three circles of polystyrene in graduating sizes. Thread these on a length of brass rod with a wooden bead between each layer and a smaller one for the very top. Let the rod protrude at the base.

FIXING TREES AND HEDGES

When fixing trees make them removable for cleaning the garden and transporting. By using a fairly substantial baseboard, say ¼in (6mm), you can drill holes in it to take the brass rods of the trees. Alternatively, raise the board off the table with a small plinth.

The same principle can be used for the hedges, the arched entrance and the topiary birds on top. Glue brass rods into the bases with UHU or impact glue to give a firm hold. The arch and birds are merely pressed into the top of the hedge. The hedge base is slotted into holes in the baseboard.

WROUGHT-IRON GATE

For the gate I used eight curtain hooks. Place these in a pattern with a wood surround and stick together with a clear spirit glue. Add two gate posts and two mini hinges and the gate is complete.

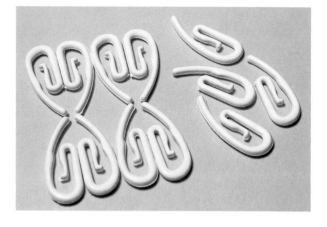

Curtain hooks were used to create a wrought-iron gate

The gate leads you under the arch and up the garden path

WOODEN GATE

1 Lay three strips of narrow stripwood as the base of your gate.

2 To these glue vertical strips which have the tops sanded to a point. On these glue only two strips, top and bottom with an angled diagonal crossbar.

3 Glue the gate between posts (chopsticks). A fence is made the same way except you do not add strips to the upper side and the sections are joined together with the main posts.

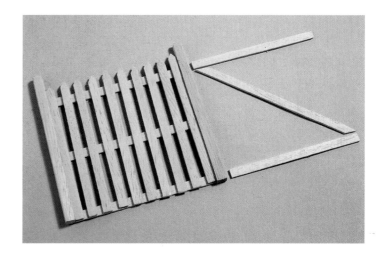

Wooden gates and fencing are easy to make from narrow stripwood

STONE BALUSTRADE

Wooden beads have many uses for the miniaturist, including newel posts on a staircase, standard lamps and stone balusters.

1 Take a small piece of brass rod and slide it into a bead. Grip the protruding rod and rub the bead across sandpaper to slightly flatten both ends. This is so they have a contact area for gluing together.

2 Thread the required beads on the brass rod so it is flush with the top and bottom beads, adding the glue as you go.

3 For the garden cut the rails from obeche wood and glue the balusters between.

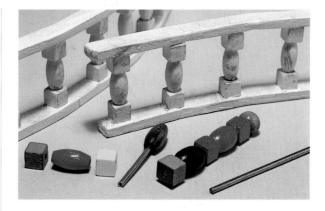

Ordinary wooden beads make 'carved' balustrades or newel posts. Thread onto a brass rod for strength

4 As with the hedges and tree, do not fix these permanently so they can be removed for cleaning the patio and can be packed away easily.

POND

Miniaturists would usually mould a pond from modelling clay. However, garden centres which sell full-size fancy-shaped garden ponds have mini samples produced by the manufacturers in plastic sheets. Most will be happy to give you some.

The ponds are mainly designed for sinking in the earth so for a miniature garden you have to make a raised area to take the chosen pond shape. The patio is made from a vinyl floor tile cut into crazy paving shapes.

The raised patio to take the sunken pond gives the garden a three dimensional feel

PLANTS

Plants from fish tank specialists or a cake-making shop are ideal. Use dried tea leaves for earth and slot all the plant stems into holes in the ground.

The long plant troughs were made from the After Eight trays as described for window-boxes (see page 125).

ORNAMENTS

Most of the furniture and ornaments were picked up from boot sales or junk shops; others I have made or adapted from broken items. A beautiful

garden doesn't have to be expensive; if you use a little ingenuity it can give a small dolls' house an extra attraction.

The dovecote was made from card and the bees outside the raffia hive are painted seeds

THE COMPLETED HOUSE

This is the completed house. I shall continue to work on it
as inspiration dictates. It needs to look more realistic with weathered
paintwork and by adding a mock staircase to the loft. This will consist of
two false doors and a box on the outside. I still have to make wood floors for
the loft bedroom and sitting-room and, of course, it must have lighting.
Redesigning a roughly-made kit in an inferior wood has been a
challenge but the result is reasonable for a town house. I hope you will be even more
satisfied with the result of your own dolls' house. Have a happy time furnishing it.

ABOUT THE AUTHOR

In 1989 Beryl Armstrong was looking for a new hobby. While admiring a fellow writer's new dolls' house she decided that was the challenge she needed. Without previous knowledge, experience or books, she bought pieces of wood and by trial and error, her first dolls' house, West Green Manor, evolved.

Beryl's main interests lie in architecture, lighting and the challenge of creating new ideas at minimal cost.

She has been writing for several dolls' house magazines over the last 11 years, and this is her second book. A selection of her many houses can often be seen at exhibitions and she shares her experience and skills giving talks to a variety of clubs. Beryl lives in West Sussex, England.

INDEX